The
OXFORDSHIRE
Way
A WALKER'S GUIDE

*Edited by Faith Cooke and
Keith Wheal
Cartography by Gavin Thomas*

D1189054

OXFORDSHIRE
COUNTY COUNCIL
CULTURAL SERVICES

New edition published in 1999 by Oxfordshire County Council
First published in 1993 by Oxfordshire Books

Copyright © Oxfordshire County Council 1993

All rights reserved. No part of this publication may be reproduced,
stored in a retrieval system, or transmitted, in any form, or by any
means, electronic, mechanical, photocopying, recording or otherwise,
without the prior permission of the publishers and copyright holder

British Library Cataloguing in Publication Data. A catalogue record for
this book is available from the British Library

Library of Congress Cataloging in Publication Data applied for

Oxfordshire County Council
Cultural Services
Holton
Oxford
OX33 1QQ

ISBN 1-900478-01-3
(previously published by
Alan Sutton Publishing Ltd
under ISBN 0-7509-0356-2)

Typeset in 10/12 Times
Typesetting and origination by
Alan Sutton Publishing Limited
Printed in Great Britain by
Information Press, Eynsham, Oxford OX8 1JJ

Contents

THE OXFORDSHIRE WAY

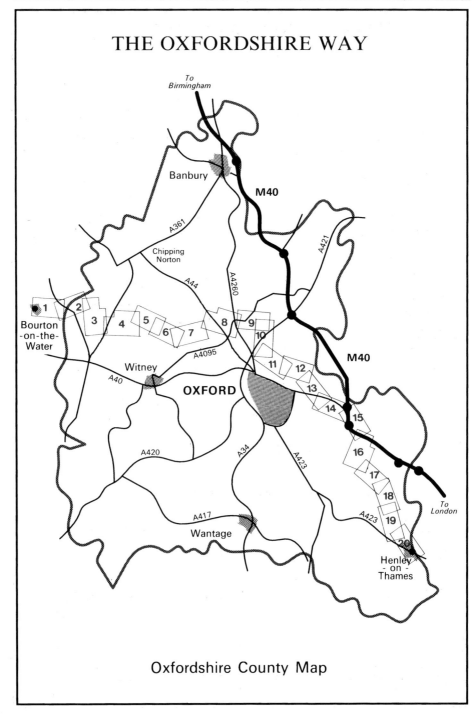

Oxfordshire County Map

THE OXFORDSHIRE WAY
Route Sections

1. Bourton-on-the-Water to Gawcombe Woods
2. Gawcombe Woods to Bledington
3. Bledington to Shipton-under-Wychwood
4. Shipton-under-Wychwood to Catsham Lane
5. Catsham Lane to Charlbury
6. Charlbury to Stonesfield
7. Stonesfield to Wootton Door
8. Wootton Door to Kirtlington
9. Kirtlington to Weston-on-the-Green
10. Weston-on-the-Green to Islip
11. Islip to Beckley
12. Beckley to Menmarsh Guide Post
13. Menmarsh Guide Post to Waterperry
14. Waterperry to Rycote
15. Rycote to Tetsworth
16. Tetsworth to Pyrton
17. Pyrton to Christmas Common
18. Christmas Common to Pishill
19. Pishill to Middle Assendon
20. Middle Assendon to Henley-on-Thames

Key to Maps

———— Oxfordshire Way

----- Other Rights of Way

✚	Place of Worship	SCH	School
PH	Public House	T	Telephone
PO	Post Office	P	Parking
Liby	Library	✚	Site of Antiquity

Scale

Kilometres   1   2   3
0
Miles   1   2

Foreword

I am proud to be invited to write the foreword to this new edition of the guide to the Oxfordshire Way. It is just fifteen years since the Oxfordshire Branch of the council for the Protection of Rural England (CPRE) produced and published the first guide to the Oxfordshire Way. It was fitting that it should do so; the Oxfordshire Way was imagined, explored, trodden out, surveyed and mapped by CPRE, with the help of many friends in amenity societies and lasting support from the County Council, the District Councils, and the Cotswold Wardens Service.

Much has changed since then, but the peace and beauty of the Oxfordshire countryside remains. More traffic, on ever bigger roads, fewer stone walls and hedgerows, and development creeping out into green fields have between them struck some deadly blows, but the route, deliberately chosen by CPRE to link fieldpath to fieldpath right across the county, has preserved its integrity as a sixty-five mile country walk. There are still breathtaking views, remote farms, downland turf and lark song. Now, adopted by the County Council and regarded as a Regional Route, considerable effort is put into its maintenance but, at the same time, great care taken not to spoil its character by overdoing waymarking or being too zealous over general improvements.

You should not lose your way on the Oxfordshire Way nowadays, but you may still get muddy feet, still need to slash back the occasional nettle, still wish that blackberries did not have to grow on such very prickly brambles so very close to the path. In other words, you will still be taking a real country walk through the lovely county of Oxfordshire. I hope it is a walk you will very much enjoy.

Alison Kemp
Vice President and Joint Chairman
Council for the Protection of Rural England,
Oxfordshire Branch

In memory of
Roland Pomfret.

Introduction

The Oxfordshire Way is a sixty-five mile recreational walk which runs south-east from Bourton-on-the-Water to Henley-on-Thames. The route passes through the most rural and scenic landscapes of Oxfordshire, including two Areas of Outstanding Natural Beauty: the Cotswolds, with their characteristic grey limestone buildings and walls; and the Chilterns, with their flint and brick architecture and famous beech woods.

Following the Oxfordshire Way

Whether you are a serious walker wishing to walk the route in one go, or a more casual walker looking for an afternoon's or day's walk, this guide will help you follow and enjoy the Oxfordshire Way. The route has been split into easy walking distances, allowing you to select particular stretches if you wish. Each walk section has descriptive written directions which can be used together with the sketch maps provided alongside. On the ground the Oxfordshire Way is signposted in both directions each time the route leaves a metalled road, and is fully waymarked.

Choose your walking distance
Each walk gives you an indication of approximate mileage covered by that particular section of the Oxfordshire Way. There is also a cumulative total for your information should you have begun at Bourton-on-the-Water in order to walk the whole route.

Easy access to the route
Each section of the walk begins and ends in or near a village or town. The larger centres like Charlbury, Stonesfield, Woodstock, Islip, Tetsworth and Watlington on the whole provide local services such as transport, refreshments and accommodation. Parking space is often limited in smaller villages, and other services are often non-existent.

Points of interest
To increase your enjoyment and understanding of the landscape through which you pass, the guide details points of interest such as snippets of local history and excellent viewpoints. These descriptions are printed in brown.

1

Using the Oxfordshire Way

The Oxfordshire Way uses existing public rights of way throughout. Apart from those described and mapped in this guide you will notice that the sketch maps also show rights of way which intersect the main route. These may be used, for example, to shorten your walk or create your own circular route.

Remember that you are sharing these rights of way with other users, and most of the land over which you are passing is farmed and privately owned. Therefore treat the land with respect, keeping to the public rights of way at all times.

Follow the Country Code
Enjoy the countryside and respect its life and work.
Guard against all risk of fire.
Fasten all gates.
Keep your dogs under close control.
Keep to public paths across farmland.
Use gates and stiles to cross fences, hedges and walls.
Leave livestock, crops and machinery alone.
Take your litter home.
Help to keep all water clean.
Protect wildlife, plants and trees.
Take special care on country roads.
Make no unnecessary noise.

Put your feet first
The Oxfordshire Way passes over a variety of surfaces, so even on the least strenuous sections you are recommended to wear strong and comfortable shoes, with thick socks to prevent blisters.

For Your Information

Your Rights of Way are
Public footpaths – may be used on foot only. Sometimes waymarked in yellow.
Bridleways – may be used on foot, horseback and bicycle. Sometimes waymarked in blue.
Byways (usually old roads) and most 'Roads used as Public Paths' – may be used by all traffic.
Ordnance Survey Pathfinder and Landranger maps show most public rights of way.

On Rights of Way you can
Take a pram, pushchair or wheelchair if practicable.
Take a dog on lead or under close control.
Take a short route round an illegal obstruction or remove it sufficiently to get past.

Landowners can
Plough paths across fields – but they must normally be reinstated within two weeks, after which the paths must at all times be kept free of crops and visible on the ground.
Ask you to leave land to which you have no right of access.

Oxfordshire County Council
The Council maintains and records all rights of way, as well as developing recreational routes like the Oxfordshire Way. Obstructions, dangerous animals, harassment and misleading signs on rights of way are illegal, and should be reported to the County Council.
The Council is interested in your views on the Oxfordshire Way and this guide. Any comments or other enquiries should be addressed to:
The Countryside Service, Department of Leisure and Arts, Oxfordshire County Council, Holton, Oxford OX33 1QQ.

Other Information

Ordnance Survey maps
The sketch maps in this guide will help you to follow the Oxfordshire Way. If you need more detailed information, however, then the following Ordnance Survey map series make an excellent complement: Landranger (1:50,000); Pathfinder (1:25,000). Information shown on these maps includes viewpoints, places of interest, picnic sites, caravan and camping sites, public houses and telephones. The following sheets cover the relevant area:

Landranger
163 Cheltenham and Cirencester
164 Oxford
165 Aylesbury and Leighton Buzzard
174 Newbury and Wantage
175 Reading and Windsor
Pathfinder
SP 02/12 Winchcombe and Stow-on-the-Wold
SP 21/31 Burford and Witney (North)

SP 41/51 Woodstock
SP 60/70 Thame
SU 69/79 Watlington and Stokenchurch
SU 68/78 Henley-on-Thames and Wallingford

Staying Overnight
Accommodation information has not been provided in this guide as details can change at any given time. Should you require accommodation details it is recommended that you contact the English Tourist Board or Tourist Information Centres (TICs) close to the Oxfordshire Way. Another good source for bed and breakfast and hotel information is the Yellow Pages for the Oxford region, reference copies of which can be found in most large libraries and general post offices.

Useful Addresses
English Tourist Board, Thames Tower, Black's Road, Hammersmith, London W6 9EL
Burford TIC, The Brewery, Sheep Street, Burford, OX18 4LP. Tel (0993) 823558
Oxford TIC, St Aldates Chambers, St Aldates Street, Oxford. Tel (0865) 726871
Thame TIC, Thame Town Hall, Thame, OX9 3UP. Tel (0844) 212834
Witney TIC, Town Hall, Witney, Oxon. Tel (0993) 775802
Woodstock TIC, Caravan, Hensington Road, Woodstock, OX20 1JQ. Tel (0993) 811038

Getting There
Bus services:
These connect a number of places on the Oxfordshire Way. The majority of services are Monday to Friday, with limited routes operating on Saturdays and Sundays. To obtain information on local public transport services write to Oxfordshire County Council for area timetable books. The following are required for the Oxfordshire Way:

1 Oxford (East) and Wheatley
2 Oxford (North) and Woodstock
5 Oxfordshire Chilterns
6 Bicester
8 Chipping Norton
9 Witney

Enclose a large stamped addressed envelope (9 x 6 in) together with your list of booklets required, and send to: Oxfordshire County Council, Public Transport Section, Department of Planning and Property Services, Speedwell House, Speedwell Street, Oxford OX1 1SD.

Rail Services:
The following railway stations are close to the Oxfordshire Way:
Shipton-under-Wychwood
Charlbury
Finstock
Combe
Tackley
Islip
Henley-on-Thames

To enquire about services phone: British Rail, Park End Street, Oxford. Tel (0865) 722333.

Background

As you walk the Oxfordshire Way this guide will indicate how much of our heritage is present in the surrounding landscape. You will see the influence of man everywhere, from prehistoric tracks, Domesday Book manors and medieval woodland clearance to eighteenth-century designed landscapes, nineteenth-century fieldscapes and farms, and modern development. Wildlife can be found everywhere, often with a tale to tell about the past, and even the underlying geology has had a major influence on the landscape we see today.

Geology

The landscape is essentially dictated by the underlying rock formation. The Oxfordshire Way takes you across all five major topographical belts in the county each with its own geology: the Cotswold limestones, the Oxford clay vale, the Oxford (Corallian) Heights, the gault clay vale and finally the chalk of the Chiltern hills. Following the Oxfordshire Way from Bourton-on-the-Water to Henley you will walk over 100 million years of geology as the rocks underfoot become slowly younger.

The Great Oolite limestone (Cotswold stone) was formed by the deposition of numerous spherical particles of calcium carbonate in the warm shallow sea which covered this part of Britain in the Jurassic period (195–136 million years ago). Fossilized seashells may be seen in some walls in the area. Variations on this limestone include forest marble, a harder building stone, and Stonesfield slate, a sandy limestone which was split to make roofing slates.

The Cotswolds are drained by rivers like the Evenlode and Glyme which have deposited alluvial soils in their valley bottoms. Early settlers found these ideal for hay meadows, while the limestone uplands were suitable for grazing pasture and woodland.

The 4 square mile plain of Otmoor lies in the Oxford clay vale. This thick, stiff clay is rich in organic matter and was deposited when the area was covered by a deep, still sea. For centuries Otmoor was a swamp ringed by rough pasture. To the south lie the Oxford Heights which rise to 125 m (400 ft) at Beckley. This ridge of higher land is composed of Corallian sands, limestones and small coral reefs formed when the deeper muddy seas gave way to clear shallow water again.

Beyond the Oxford Heights the Oxfordshire Way crosses the wide gault clay vale over which the River Thame has laid great spreads of river gravels. Ahead lies the escarpment of the Chiltern hills, composed of chalk which is overlain on the hill tops by clay with flint and sometimes sand and gravel. Chalk is made up of the remains of microscopic marine creatures with calcite (calcium-based) skeletons which were deposited in a shallow sea, eventually forming thick layers of chalk. This happened about 100 million years ago in the Cretaceous period. Within the chalk are bands of flints which are formed from silica, with a dark coloured inside and a white coating. This geology is evident in the traditional brick and flint buildings of the Chilterns, which make use of readily available materials.

Chalk allows water to pass down through it. Along the bottom of the escarpment there are numerous springs where this water meets the impermeable gault clay and greensand. This difference in the geology affected early settlement patterns and the springline is marked by a string of settlements, like Shirburn and Pyrton, whose sites were chosen because of the ready supply of water.

About 26 million years ago, as the continental plates of Africa and Europe collided, forming the Alps, the layers of rock now making up south-east England buckled. A series of east–west folds were formed, including those we now know as the Cotswolds and Chilterns.

The Past in the Landscape

Fields and Hedges

In the fields some sign of the past can still be seen. In places where there has been long undisturbed pasture there may be remnants of ridge-and-furrow cultivation dating back to the open-field system of the Middle Ages. Each village had some form of open field farming, with two or three huge fields divided into furlongs, which were further subdivided into strips held by tenants. Each individual held land scattered throughout the fields, so good or poor conditions were shared. Crops were grown in a two- or three-year rotation, details differing from place to place, so each year one field would lie fallow or unsown to allow the soil to rest and to get rid of weeds. The fallow field would provide grazing for animals as would the other fields after harvest. The land was ploughed in such a way as to produce high ridges of soil from which water would drain into the dividing furrows. In the fourteenth century some arable land was laid down to pasture after the reduction in the work-force due to the Black Death, and these ridges and furrows were grassed over, still remaining visible in some places.

In the Chilterns and other wooded areas a different agricultural landscape evolved. People lived in isolated hamlets, their fields carved out of the woodland over the years, a process called 'assarting'. Instead of large open fields, these were smaller, more numerous and enclosed by hedges formed from remnants of woodland. Some of these fields were farmed in common by tenants, crops being rotated in a similar way to those on the large open fields, while others were owned either by the lord of the manor or by individual farmers.

Enclosure

By Tudor times (the sixteenth century) some tenants in the open fields were beginning to amalgamate their strips to make cultivation easier, and gradually this move away from the open field system was seen to be a more efficient way to farm. New legume and fodder crops and better rotation improved the soil quality so that by the mid-eighteenth century major landowners were imposing a new system of smaller, regular shaped and hedged fields on their land. New farms were built, often away from the village, roads were realigned and the old common land was turned into agricultural land. This led to social upheaval in many places, the smallholders losing their land in the reorganization and becoming labourers on the large farms. At first this enclosure was organized by agreement of all concerned, and later by private acts of parliament for particular parishes. Later in the nineteenth century there was a General Enclosure Act, which contained more safeguards for the poor such as the provision of allotments to mitigate the effect of the loss of common land.

In contrast to these rich woodland hedges, the enclosure hedges of the eighteenth and nineteenth centuries tend to have only one or two species, usually hawthorn or blackthorn, and have no woodland plants. These hedges were planted as a result of the enclosure acts, when the large open fields, still with individual strips, were divided into rectangular plots to improve crop yields and to consolidate land holdings. Earlier than this, some landowners enclosed their holdings on the open field, using a mixture of trees or shrubs taken from nearby woodland. Hedges planted originally with a single species can be dated approximately: in a 30-yard stretch each species of tree or woody shrub is equivalent to 100 years in age. However, many factors can influence the number of species, so for an accurate date this biological information should be confirmed by documentary evidence.

Enclosure transformed the wide open vistas with few hedges into neat, ordered countryside with miles of new hawthorn hedges planted at the landowners' expense to make the new fields. Since the Second World War many of these hedges have been grubbed up to allow easy access for large modern machinery, the landscape changing yet again with much public outcry, this time from conservationists.

Common hawthorn

Boundaries

Parish boundaries are thought to date back to Roman or Iron Age estates, and Anglo-Saxon charters still exist for some parishes, describing the bounds which can still be traced on the ground. These important administrative boundaries often follow natural features such as watercourses or hilltop ridges, while man-made hedges, ditches and banks, although probably constructed after the definition of the parish, follow the boundary to take a characteristically sinuous line over the countryside. Roads and paths often follow boundaries, either as a result of marking the bounds of a parish or else because a through route was taken between the territories of two land units.

In woodland, banks are often seen. They mark boundaries of coppice areas (as in Wychwood Forest), divisions of ownership or can show the position of an earlier woodland edge, especially if the composition of the woodland is different on each side. The banks are usually associated with a ditch. If the ditch is on the woodland side of the bank, then this was designed to prevent the escape of deer from the wood and possibly indicates the earlier existence of a deer park.

Roads and Tracks

Many of the roads in the area have always been used as such. Some have increased in importance over the centuries, while others have declined and are now no more than paths or grassy tracks.

From Stonesfield to Tackley, for example, the Oxfordshire Way follows Akeman Street. This ancient track was incorporated by the Romans into their road network to link Verulamium (St Albans) and Corinium (Cirencester). As a result there was a strong Roman presence in the area, with villas at North Leigh and Stonesfield occupied until the early fifth century AD by members of the British governing class, not Roman immigrants.

To the east of Watlington the Oxfordshire Way crosses the Icknield Way, reputed to be one of the oldest routes in England – at least 4,000 years old. It originally linked Wessex and East Anglia and took its name from a later tribe, the Iceni, to whose territory it led. Originally it was not a marked track but a wide belt up to a mile in width, which mostly kept to the fairly well-drained lower chalk at the base of the hills.

In the intervening centuries the Icknield Way has gradually been narrowed and formalized by settlement and agriculture, and is now three parallel routes that can clearly be seen on an Ordnance Survey map. The Upper and Lower Icknield Ways were used as drove roads up to the nineteenth century, when the enclosure awards reduced them to bridleways. The Upper Icknield Way is still a long-distance path, now for recreation rather than for communication, and takes its modern name, the Ridgeway, from the section along the top of the Berkshire Downs.

Natural History

Ancient Woodland

The natural vegetation in southern England, had it been left undisturbed, would now be woodland. After the end of the Ice Age, about ten thousand years ago, 'wild wood' covered much of the country, but owing to man's increasing impact over the centuries it was cleared in most places to make way for settled agriculture. The remaining woodland areas were managed to provide useful timber. Descendants from the original woodland are called primary ancient woodland and are rare. Some present-day woodland has grown up in places which at some time in the past has been cleared; if it dates from before 1600 it is called secondary ancient woodland. More recent woods are called secondary woodland. Interestingly it is estimated that the area of woodland cover today is roughly what it was during the Roman occupation.

Most old areas of woodland were managed in the past by selective felling and coppicing, which is the periodic cutting of the trees to ground level. New growth springs up, producing within a few years wood suitable for fencing, firewood or repairs. Wychwood, for example, was divided into compartments which were coppiced over an eighteen-year cycle and then fenced to keep out grazing animals, particularly deer and domestic sheep, goats, pigs and cattle, so as to allow new shoots to grow and provide the next supply of underwood. The most common coppice tree was hazel, which was used for wattle fencing as it is so pliable, while oak and ash were common standard trees in this area. The continuity of woodland has resulted in the development of specific communities of plants which can thrive in the shady conditions, or which flourish in years of light conditions brought about by coppicing. Plants which can only spread slowly are good indicators of ancient woodland, for example wood anemone, spurge laurel, yellow archangel, primrose and goldilocks buttercup. Certain trees and shrubs are also characteristic of ancient woodland, for example field maple, midland hawthorn and service tree. In order to identify ancient woodland by its vegetation many such species need to be present. In places which were once thickly wooded but are now cleared, some of these indicator species persist in hedges formed from

Wood anemone

11

unfelled woodland strips. These give a clue to the age of the hedge, if the date of the woodland felling is known.

Coppicing died out before the last war, but is being revived in some places especially as a means of wildlife conservation. It produces a variety of habitats during the cycle of cutting and regrowth, thus allowing flowering plants to flourish during the open phase, which is then suppressed when the tree cover is dense. Various birds and insects favour different aspects of the cycle as well, some liking scrubby conditions while others prefer a more open habitat.

Yellow archangel

Beech Woodland

The most striking characteristic of the Chiltern hills is their beech woods. Beech is a native British tree which became widespread in woodland about two and a half thousand years ago, south of a line between the Wash and south Wales. In the past other species such as oak and ash would have been more numerous, but it seems likely that beech was dominant especially on the chalky slopes. Although some experts maintain that all the beech woods were planted for the nineteenth-century furniture industry in High Wycombe, medieval records, like those from Cuxham, point to the plentiful supply of beech. Early travellers like John Leland and Daniel Defoe in the sixteenth and seventeenth centuries describe the Chiltern beech woods, emphasizing their main use – providing fuel for London by means of coppicing.

As the need for firewood decreased owing to the availability of coal, so beech became the staple for a new local industry, that of furniture making, and management changed to produce timber instead of coppice wood. Over a period of about a century the best trees were felled on a selective basis and used for making the legs and stretchers for Windsor and other chairs, which were produced on a large scale in the High Wycombe and Stokenchurch areas.

Therefore beech was actively encouraged for the furniture trade, and seeds and saplings were set to replace felled trees. However, over a long period of time the best trees were used, so those that remain today tend to be less healthy or poor specimens; this is one reason why these beautiful woods are under threat.

Beech woods are very different from mixed woodland. The trees produce a dense shade and deep leaf litter so that the ground flora tends to be patchy or in some places non-existent, especially where the soil is very flinty and the ground is too dry. Shade-tolerant trees and shrubs like holly, yew and spurge laurel grow in some places, while in others brambles cover the ground, few flowering in the deep shade. The smaller flowering plants are all those which flower in the spring before

Spurge laurel

the leaf cover is too thick. Many of the ancient woodland indicator species mentioned above can be found especially in glades or along paths.

Two other plants to look out for which have evolved different methods of coping with the poor light conditions are dog's mercury and the well-known bluebell, a common sight in the beech woods. Dog's mercury flowers very early in the season with green flowers pollinated by insects. Plants are either male or female, but also spread by underground stems or rhizomes. The leaves are present almost all year and persist in the driest summers, even though they may wilt, lasting to the end of the following winter. This strategy gives maximum efficiency in producing food by photosynthesis. Bluebells overcome the problem of shade by having a different life cycle. The bulbs sprout very early in the winter so that the plant can take advantage of the light afforded by the leafless conditions above. By the time the beech is fully in leaf, the bluebells have flowered, set seed and become dormant for the summer, the seeds germinating the following winter. Bluebells are not necessarily woodland plants but cannot tolerate much competition from vigorous grasses and plants or trampling from animals, so have taken refuge in a habitat which is not really adequate but which affords them some protection.

Cotswold Limestone Grassland

The striking characteristic of natural limestone grassland is the rich flora, that provides an ideal habitat for butterflies. The soil contains much calcium but few other nutrients, and is porous, tending to dry out quickly, so that tall grasses are restricted thus allowing other plants to flourish. These plants can tolerate the calcareous conditions (calcicole plants) and often have adaptations such as hairy leaves to help reduce water loss. Many belong to the pea family (legumes), clovers, vetches, bird's foot trefoil, meddick and sainfoin, all of which can fix nitrogen from the air, so improving their nutrition.

Another factor in the formation of rich limestone grassland is the action of centuries of sheep grazing, which produced a short turf, but now that the sheep are no longer so dominant in the agricultural scene, and myxomatosis has reduced the rabbit population, this type of grassland is becoming threatened by scrub encroachment. The widespread use of artificial fertilizers stimulates the growth of coarse grasses and larger herbs which dominate the smaller flowery plants, so that in many places the only limestone grassland flora which remains is on steep slopes and unsprayed roadside verges.

Chilterns Chalk Grassland
It used to be thought that areas of open chalk grassland had never been covered with wildwood, but more recent evidence seems to show that woodland was present. Neolithic (New Stone Age) man gradually started to clear the forest about four and a half thousand years ago, the areas of chalk being easier to cultivate than heavy clay soil elsewhere. By the end of the Iron Age, two and a half thousand years later, both arable cultivation and intensive sheep grazing were taking place on the chalk slopes. When agriculture became less intensive after the departure of the Romans a proportion of the Chiltern grassland reverted to beech wood, but other areas remained open and were used throughout the Middle Ages for sheep and cattle grazing.

Rock rose

Chalk grassland is a semi-natural habitat produced by the action of grazing, which prevents the growth of scrub and woodland. It is characteristically rich in flowers, which flourish owing to the lack of competition from tall grasses that cannot thrive when grazed or in poor soil and dry conditions.

Many plants show adaptations to cope with these conditions. Some, like salad burnet and lady's bedstraw, have very long root systems, advantageous when the top soil dries out. Others, often members of the daisy family, conserve water by having hairy leaves or by pressing their leaves close to the ground, often forming a rosette – adaptations which at the same time reduce the effects of grazing.

Chalk grassland is managed today by careful sheep grazing to retain this mixture of flowers, and this goes hand in hand with maintaining an associated rich variety of animals and insects, conspicuous among which are butterflies and moths.

Anthills, made by colonies of yellow ants, are a feature of old grassland and show by their size how long the grassland has remained undisturbed. The soil particles are small and after a time the original flora is buried. A characteristic plant community develops with such plants as forget-me-not and wall speedwell, annuals which produce many seeds to recolonize during the next season, while thyme and rock rose are perennials which can tolerate burial as the ants build up the mould.

Acknowledgements

These background notes are taken from the Oxfordshire Country Walks series (1. *Evenlode and Wychwood*; 2. *Chilterns*; 3. *Otmoor*) written and researched by Mary Webb, Alan Spicer and Allister Smith, all of the Oxford Brookes University.

If you enjoy walking the Oxfordshire Way, the circular walks in these three books (many of which use part of the Oxfordshire Way) will help you to explore more of the surrounding countryside.

We would like to thank the following for providing illustrations: the Centre for Oxfordshire Studies: pp. 20, 24, 25, 30, 34, 35, 40, 48, 49, 53, 59, 63, 66, 71, 74; Danny Perry: pp. 21, 31, 42, 82; Louise Spicer: pp. 9, 11, 12, 14, 56, 67. Thanks are also due to the cartographer, Gavin Thomas.

Bourton-on-the-Water to Bledington

Passing through Wyck Rissington

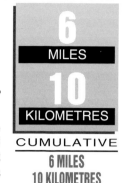

6 MILES

10 KILOMETRES

CUMULATIVE

6 MILES

10 KILOMETRES

The Way begins on a narrow roadway at an Oxfordshire Way signpost, with the model railway exhibition on the left, and leads to a tarmac footpath with a sign, starting off between a large stone house on the left and an ornamental gateway on the right. The footpath soon meets another. Turn left along this and then almost immediately right, continuing with the allotments on your left and then car-parks on either side. At the road by the health centre cross over to Roman Way, and take Moor Lane with Harp Farm House on your left.

Through the hedge on your right lies an Iron Age hill-fort, Salmondsbury Camp, with its massive earthworks. The site covers about 60 acres.

Continue along Moor Lane, which gradually becomes a farm track, until you reach a fork. The left track goes to Moor Lane Farm, but you should bear sharply to the right, south-east, along the hedged lane. Do not go as far as the gate at the end, but look for a field-gate and a kissing gate on your left, opposite which is a field-gate on your right. Turn left here entering the water meadows. Keep the old high hedge on your left and proceed over the level and, at times, boggy meadow to two small concrete water tanks near the foot-bridge over the River Eye. Cross the field to a foot-bridge over a ditch. This ditch is the old course of the River Dikler, and is the parish boundary between Bourton-on-the-Water and Wyck Rissington.

A small grass field leads to a foot-bridge over the very fast-flowing little River Dikler. This is the site of Wyck Mill, now vanished, with lovely wild flowers growing beside the clear water. Carry straight on, over the hillock, and eastwards to a field-gate and concrete bridge over a stream. Beyond this you cross a small grass field to a wire fence. Turn left and follow the fence, with a tree plantation on the left of the narrow field, at the end of which is a field-gate and a flat bridge over the ditch. A grass track with stream and hedge on the right takes you to a field-gate on to the village road opposite Wyck Rissington postbox. Here

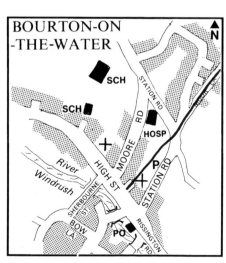

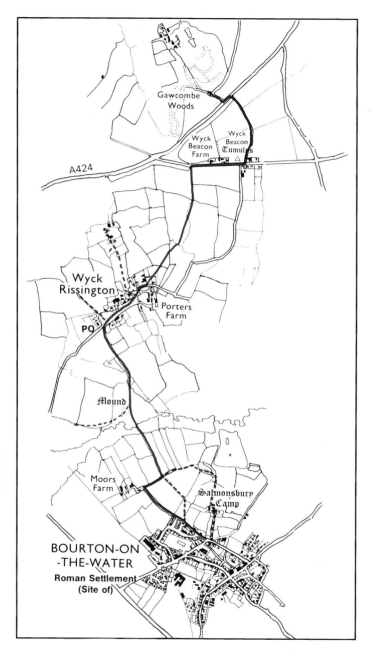

17

bear right.

Having walked up the village street to the church go through the gate into the churchyard, keeping immediately left of the church, and go to a kissing gate. Cross the cart-track and the stile; proceed over the field to a foot-bridge. Bear right here and cross the next two fields, then follow the path uphill, turning right half-way up, to a gap in the hedge and a stream crossing. In several of the fields around you can see clear signs of the old strip farming.

Climb steadily up, with hedge and stream, spring and trough all on your left, to a stile beside a gate. Keep to the right of the hedge, carrying on steeply uphill along a well-used track to a gap in the hedge. The track takes you out on to a metalled road just beside a small open barn. You have climbed to about 800 feet above sea level and it is worth pausing to look back at the panoramic view below.

Turn right along the road and then left down the bridleway opposite Court Hayes Riding School on the right. In the field on your left is Wyck Beacon, a 6 feet high round barrow. All around are wide views – across the Windrush valley to the high Cotswolds; Bourton-on-the-Water below you, and Stow-on-the-Wold on its hilltop to the north. Over to the right, a field away, you can see the houses of RAF Rissington. The path enters a small belt of trees and emerges, through a field-gate, on to the A424. This is one of England's loveliest ridge routes. All the way from Burford to Stow one enjoys glorious views of the Cotswold hills on both sides of the road, and the grass verges, in late summer, are a carpet of flowers. The A424 is virtually the watershed between the Windrush and the Evenlode. Behind you now is the steep western scarp side of the Cotswolds; in front the dip slopes of the Evenlode valley. A great deal of West Oxfordshire lies spread out before you; Wychwood Forest, the spire and radio masts of Leafield, and even, on a clear day, the valleys of the Windrush and the Thames.

Turn left along the A424 for a few yards until you are opposite the Westcote turn. Cross over and walk down here until the road turns sharply right. You carry straight on, past a lodge on your left. The drive goes steeply down between woodlands and ornamental trees, the verges a mass of flowers. Follow the drive right down to the entrance to Gawcombe House. The ornamental lakes are below you on your right, and in spring a host of daffodils capped by a view of the Forest of Wychwood is on the horizon. Gawcombe House itself was rebuilt about the middle of the last century, but has interesting ancillary buildings, including a stable yard and a dovecot. Keep on down the drive between these buildings, bearing right under the archway, and then left on to a clearly defined cart-track. As you go down this track you can enjoy fine

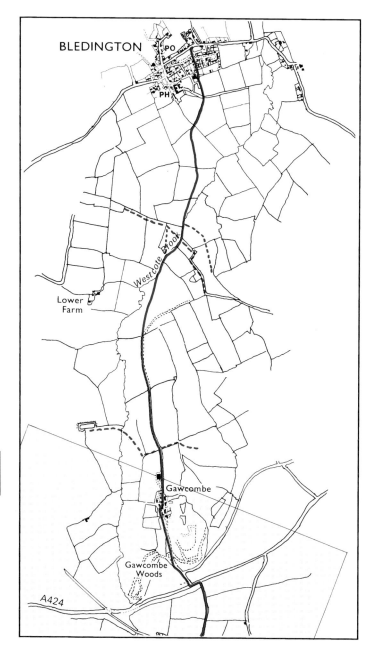

views of Daylesford (birthplace and burial-place of Warren Hastings), Kingham Hill, and the church towers of Chipping Norton, Kingham, Bledington and Churchill, the last being a scaled-down copy of Magdalen College tower. Continue downhill along a wide cart-track through two fields, after which you come to a field which gradually narrows to a strip, with a stream on the right, then a bank, and finally a substantial bridle-bridge over Westcote Brook.

Crossing the bridge turn right, with the brook on your right, and after a short distance there is a gap in the hedge. The Oxfordshire Way continues alongside Westcote Brook, passing a bridle-bridge on the left, over a track, to a foot-bridge going off to your right. Here you gradually leave the stream, going due east across a field to a stile. You have to cross another field, to a point just south of a row of tree stumps that mark a bridge. Yet another field lies ahead; you veer left, north-east, to a field-gate, a wide wooden bridge and a bridge with a stile.

In the next field climb uphill with the hedge on your left and a wind-pump on your right, to a stile that takes you into a lane. Cross the lane, go over two stiles, along a well-worn path to yet another stile and then along a path running down the centre of a little burial ground to the metalled road. Continue past modern housing to the main road where you turn right towards the county boundary. From here on, most of the fields will seem larger and you may have fewer stiles to climb than in the quiet corner of Gloucestershire you are about to leave.

Wyck Rissington village green, c. 1920

Bourton-on-the-Water

Bourton-on-the-Water

Bourton-on-the-Water is in the Cotswolds, and on the great Roman road, the Fosse Way, which has become today one of England's best scenic through routes. It has a great many beautiful stone houses, cottages of various periods and a most interesting church, rebuilt in the nineteenth century but incorporating a fourteenth-century chancel and a Georgian tower. The River Windrush is the real start of the Oxfordshire Way, though it will reach the Thames long before you do; and you will meet several more of the equally lovely rivers flowing into the Thames, notably the Evenlode and the Cherwell.

Wyck Rissington

Wyck Rissington is a lovely unspoilt village which seems hardly to have changed for centuries. Its most charming feature is the wide expanse of village green with an attractive pond that lines both sides of the village street for much of its length. Behind the green are rows of delightful stone houses and cottages, mostly dating from the seventeenth and eighteenth centuries. The church is well worth a visit, especially as your path takes you right through the churchyard. It contains, among many interesting features, some carved wooden plaques depicting the life of Christ, thought to be sixteenth-century Flemish work, and discovered towards the end of the last century at Wyck Hill House.

21

Bledington to Shipton-under-Wychwood

Passing through Bruern

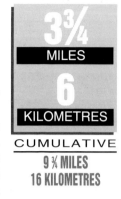

CUMULATIVE

9 ¾ MILES
16 KILOMETRES

Continue down the road, south-east, passing the turning to Kingham on your left, to the county boundary on the bridge over Westcote Brook. You are now entering the West Oxfordshire district. Turn left about 20 yards beyond the bridge through a metal gate, on a sharp right-handed bend in the road. Go across to a field-gate and then bear right uphill to a second field-gate.

You now follow the left-hand side of a hedge for nearly half a mile. The meadow slopes away on your left, affording a fine view of the Evenlode valley. At a wide gap in the hedge at the end of this great field turn left, and follow the right-hand side of the hedge to the brook at the bottom of the field; turn right again, and follow the right bank of the brook to a little stone bridge just short of its junction with the river Evenlode. Turn right at this bridge, and go up across the field to a track through a belt of trees. This leads to the road through Foxholes Farm.

Turn up towards Foxholes Farm but do not go as far as the road. Instead, about 10 yards in, turn left, opposite the Oxfordshire Way signpost, down a narrow path through a wood.

Continue through the wood on a clear but very narrow track until you come to a clearing, with a track down from the right and a notice about the Berkshire, Buckinghamshire and Oxfordshire Naturalist Trust (BBONT), which has a nature reserve here. Carry straight on through the wood to a bridlegate. You will see Cocksmoor Copse on your right, and will soon be able to see Bruern Abbey clearly. Approach a bridlegate on to the road that leads down from the A424 to Bruern. Go straight across the road and through a bridlegate into the parkland of Bruern Abbey.

Bear left to pass between the iron palings of the garden on your left and an oblong fenced hollow, marked by a large ash tree on your right, then follow the left-hand side of a post and rail fence enclosing what looks like a disused cricket pitch with a pavilion. Go over the stile, or through the bridlegate, into a field. A clear well-used track leads straight across to

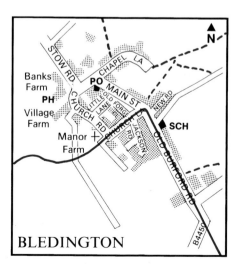

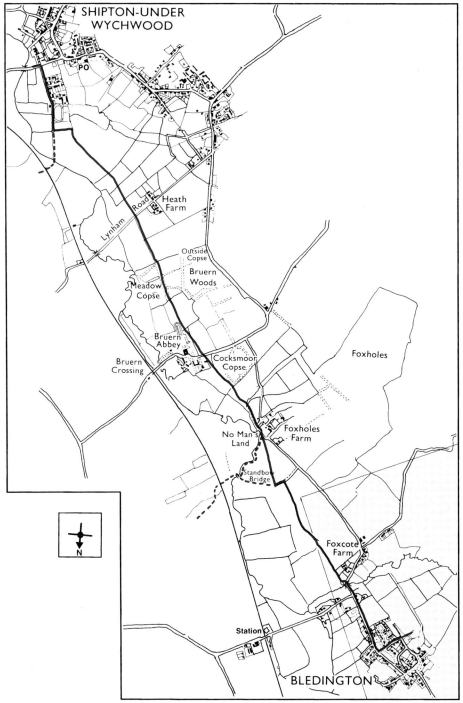

SHIPTON-UNDER
WYCHWOOD

PO

Heath
Farm

Lynham

Road

Outside
Copse

Bruern
Woods

Meadow
Copse

Bruern
Abbey

Cocksmoor
Copse

Foxholes

Bruern
Crossing

No Man's
Land

Foxholes
Farm

Standbow
Bridge

N

Foxcote
Farm

Station

BLEDINGTON

23

a bridlegate into a broad ride through Bruern Woods. Right at the far end of the ride is a wooden seat, beautifully placed to afford a view of the garden front of Bruern Abbey. Turn left at the seat and take a little tunnel through the very edge of the wood to a bridlegate. This is good open country, with the wide views over the Evenlode valley and across to Leafield radio station, with Shipton-under-Wychwood church standing out delightfully, dead ahead in the middle distance. In the next field the hedge has been removed, but the field boundary, marked by a vigorous growth of bracken, is easy to follow. Over to the left you can see the strangely incongruous warehouse at Shipton railway station, a huge three-storey red-brick edifice, a reminder that Shipton was once an important stopping place on the line.

Follow the field boundary as it curves right, then at a hedge corner turn left on to a good cart-track and follow the hedge downhill to Meadow Lane. Turn right into the lane, and continue straight on past modern housing to the A361, in Shipton-under-Wychwood.

Bledington village green in the 1930s

Rick-building, c. 1915

Bledington

Bledington is an attractive open village with pleasant old houses round a large village green and an exceptionally interesting church, with magnificent fifteenth-century clerestory, windows and glass. All the masonry is of very high quality.

Shipton-under-Wychwood to Charlbury

Passing through Ascott-under-Wychwood

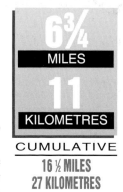

MILES

6¾

11

KILOMETRES

CUMULATIVE

16½ MILES
27 KILOMETRES

Turn left along the A361 towards Chipping Norton, cross the Evenlode and the railway, and start up the hill on the far side of the valley. Just by the entrance to the last house on the right is the beginning of the bridleway. It appears to be a private drive, but double hedgerows line the track ahead and a gate opens on to a field divided by the railway line. All the way to Charlbury the Oxfordshire Way is to share the valley with the River Evenlode and the Cotswold line. The track, easy to follow, goes close to the river and then across the railway line at a level crossing. Langley Mill lies beyond the winding river, set in the angle of an ancient weir enclosed by willows. Mill stream and river meet again at Coldstream Farm, in Shipton parish, where a large brick kiln beside the stone farmhouse shows it to be a pottery. You have now reached the western end of Ascott-under-Wychwood, known as Ascott Earl.

Go over the level crossing and across the Evenlode. At the top of the lane turn left into Ascott Earl. At the T-junction turn left, past Manor Farm and immediately after crossing the Evenlode river turn right onto a bridleway. Look for the grassy terraces and hollows between here and the river bank – all that remains of the motte-and-bailey of centuries ago. At the Evenlode bridge bear right, crossing broad fields not far from the hedge. At the end of this a bridleway sign points you on towards the ditch that marks the parish boundary with Chilson. Go through the gate and follow the hedge on your right all the way round the bottom edge of the field and up the further slope to a hunting gate beneath a thorn tree. Below, to your right, runs the Evenlode, and beyond it Ascott Mill. No longer in use as a mill, it has been converted to a pleasing private house in a delightful riverside setting. Beyond the bridlegate continue straight on up, leaving a barn on the summit to your left. A little way beyond the barn a gate leads on to a

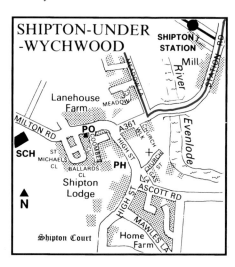

SHIPTON-UNDER-WYCHWOOD

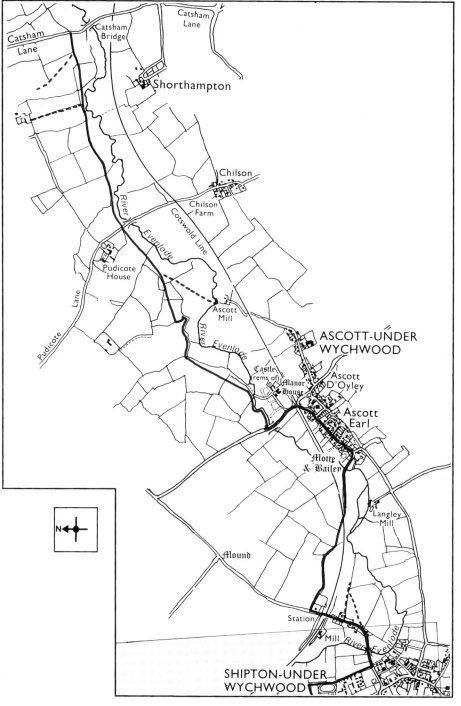

track that takes you into the parkland of Pudlicote House and out into Pudlicote Lane.

Cross Pudlicote Lane and go through a bridlegate.

At the field boundary a gate opens on to a narrow field, the river swirling away to the south, and only the intermittent willows in the foreground revealing its course. Carry on through level fields to the right of the hedgerow, but look for a small right-hand hook into the corner of a field as you draw level with the village of Shorthampton on the far side of the river towards the Forest of Wychwood. A gate and culvert a dozen yards from the corner take you into the last field before Catsham Lane.

Cross Catsham Lane, go through the bridlegate on to a narrow, well-used track, and through a gate into pasture. Suddenly one has a feeling of time standing still. A stream bubbles from the shelter of the woods to the north and runs between soft grassy banks to the swift-flowing river. A little stone bridge invites you to sit and dangle weary feet in the bright water or cool a tepid flask in its gravelly bed. It is a grand place for a rest, for from now on the path goes over hilly ground. Almost immediately you begin climbing up the field behind Greenhill Copse, following the left-hand hedge over the hill and down the other side to the ditch and hedge. A little way to your right, half hidden in the trees, is a farm gate and a bridge, a delightful little crossroads of ancient country ways. The bridleway goes straight on up to Spelsbury, but the Oxfordshire Way turns right, following the edge of the next field to Dene Grove Wood and then along the edge of the wood bank to a stile in the corner of the field.

The Oxfordshire Way then goes south-east down a pleasant pasture field to Coldron Brook, with a foot-bridge. Carry on across this field to a copse. Skirt the copse on its south side till you come to a stile in the hedge. Pause here and take a look at the splendid view to the south, with Walcot and its lovely complex of farm buildings across the valley a little above the railway line. Follow the edge of this field and soon turn left to a stile which leads on to a narrow lane. Nearly opposite is an old stone stile which takes you out into a field, from where Charlbury is visible on its hill across flat meadows. Go straight towards the village, over a stile, and, keeping left of a long barn,

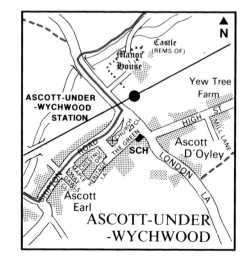

ASCOTT-UNDER
-WYCHWOOD

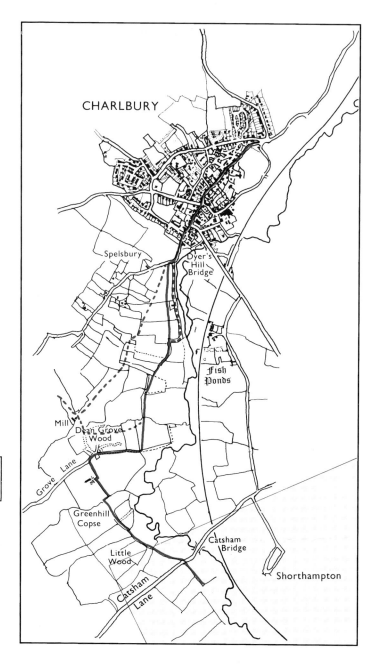

Shipton Court, c. 1920

aim for a bridge over a drainage ditch to the left of an oak tree. (A fallen stone stile lies to the right but in wet weather the ditch floods here.) Go straight on through the last field to a cattle pen and a stile. Now you are on a metalled road, the B4026. Turn right up the hill to the centre of the town.

Shipton-under-Wychwood

Shipton-under-Wychwood is a pleasant stone-built village in the Evenlode valley. There are a number of delightful old houses, many grouped round a large triangular village green, just north of which is the church, mainly dating from the thirteenth and fourteenth centuries, and with interesting features. There are two outstanding buildings, Shipton Court and the Shaven Crown Inn. Shipton Court is one of the largest early Jacobean houses in the country, built about 1603 by the Lacy family. Although it has undergone a considerable amount of modernization its essential character remains. The entrance front, facing west and visible from the A361, is most elegant and well-proportioned. The Shaven Crown, built originally as a

Shipton-under-Wychwood

hostelry, became a guest house for Bruern Abbey and later an inn, and so has a five-hundred-year-old tradition of sheltering and sustaining travellers.

Ascott-under-Wychwood

This is another pleasant stone village, with a good village green linking the two settlements of Ascott Earl and Ascott d'Oyley. The church is small and simple, mainly early thirteenth century. The manor house stands on an ancient site, within the bailey of the castle of Ascott d'Oyley, built in the middle of the twelfth century. It is mainly a sixteenth- and seventeenth-century building, but still has some medieval buttresses. Some of the original wooden mullioned windows have survived, and the farm buildings include a seventeenth-century barn with dovecot in the gable and a brick and half-timber granary standing on staddle stones. The rest of the village is a pleasant composition of stone houses and cottages of various dates.

Charlbury to Stonesfield

Leave Charlbury by Fiveways, on its southern edge, taking the Woodstock Road (B4437) past houses on either side until, after about 300 yards, the main road curves uphill to the north-east and you enter Stonesfield Lane. This begins as a gravelled lane with bungalows on your right, but soon narrows and becomes a track between hedges, through which you can catch delightful glimpses of the Evenlode, and, beyond, Cornbury Park and Wychwood forest. After half a mile you reach a gate, and cross two bridleways; continue in a south-easterly direction on a cart-track with open country on either side.

There is a fine patch of wild mignonette at the beginning of this open track. The path goes down into a small valley and then climbs up to Hill Barn Cottages. Keeping the cottages on your left continue eastwards, uphill, along a well-made farm road. After crossing another bridleway go straight on downhill and through two gateways, past farm buildings and a bungalow, to the road just west of Stonesfield village. You will already have had a fine view of the church and village from the opposite side of the valley.

Charlbury

Charlbury lies in the valley of the Evenlode; the town has grown up on the eastern bank with Cornbury Park and open farmland on the other side of the river. Originally the whole area was forested, certainly from Woodstock to the south as far as Burford to the west. Cornbury Park in fact includes a part of the ancient Wychwood forest, and the name Wychwood is also preserved in the names of the villages of Ascott, Shipton and Milton, all of them 'under Wychwood'. Charlbury is thought by some historians to have been a town (burgh) for free men (churls). It certainly became a market town as the forests were cleared and the land farmed. Tracks connected it to Enstone, Chipping Norton, Burford, Witney, Stonesfield and Woodstock; most of these tracks became the roads of today but there are several places where the old track remains and the road has

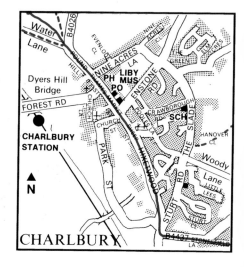

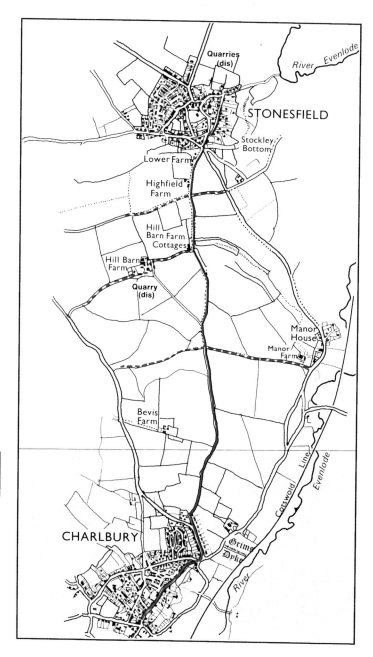

taken a different path. *The Great Western Railway arrived in 1853 and Charlbury station, thought to have been built to a design of Brunel, became an important stop on the Paddington/Worcester line. The station is now a listed building.*

The parish formed part of the Abbey of Eynsham, which at that time was in the diocese of Lincoln, but eventually the church passed to St John's College in Oxford. The church is dedicated to St Mary the Virgin; some of the Norman arches of the original building survive, but it was enlarged in the thirteenth century and restored in 1874.

Other noteworthy buildings include the Friends' Meeting House (1779), the Methodist chapel (1823) and the Baptist chapel (1823).

The centre of Charlbury is relatively unspoiled with pleasant groups of buildings all in the attractive local stone and many of them with stone-slated roofs. Almost the whole of the centre forms a conservation area. Church Street used to be the site of the market, which extended behind the Bell Hotel. Church Lane, on the other side of St Mary's, also contains some fine houses pleasantly grouped.

Not far from the centre is the Playing Close, a tree-lined green which used to be the site for village fairs. A fountain erected in 1897 was constructed by John Kibble, a very fine stonemason who was also

Charlbury: Sheep Street, c. 1925

Charlbury from the Evenlode, looking north-west, c. 1925

something of a local historian. Beyond the Playing Close most of the buildings are comparatively recent; most of the post-war development has been to the east of the town. Moving the other way from the town centre, Park Street (at the lower end of Church Street) leads quickly to open ground with Lee Place, a residence of the Duke of Marlborough, to the left and the entrance to Cornbury on the right.

Charlbury itself had a number of small farmhouses each working strips in the open fields surrounding the town. The names of some of these fields are used in naming newer streets, such as Woodfield Drive, and at least one other gives its name to the lane, Ticknell, which led to it. Sheep farming beyond the fields gave rise to the gloving industry which flourished until quite recently. Anybody interested in the history of the area should visit the small museum adjacent to the Corner House, a community building donated to the town after the war.

Stonesfield to Kirtlington

Stonesfield to Wootton Door

Coming into Stonesfield from the west you should cross over the road, and a few yards to the east take a steep gravelled bridleway going south-east, steeply uphill past a few cottages to a village road. Bear right to the Methodist chapel.

CUMULATIVE

27 ½ MILES
45 KILOMETRES

Bear right along Churchfields, passing the Parish church on your left, until the road turns sharply north. Here take the bridleway due south past a few houses and bungalows and drop very steeply down to the ford. The track is almost a series of pebble and stone steps, and as you descend you can enjoy magnificent views of the Evenlode valley. This is the place for a rest or picnic. It is one of the very few commons in north and west Oxfordshire, and is a steep hillside meadow stretching down to the river with its bathing place. The line of Akeman Street shows clearly in the turf, and the hedges are well worth examining. The one along the top of the common is at least 500 years old. The Oxfordshire Way now follows Akeman Street, so turn north-east from the ford to a nearby stile. Akeman Street then goes along a grass field to another stile, along the edge of the next field to a copse and, bearing right and left, to a gap in a stone wall. There is a good grass track along the edge of a field to another copse, and the path then goes along the top of an embankment above Baggs Bottom to a stone stile at the Stonesfield/Combe road. As you walk you will be able to see several of the old Stonesfield slate pits.

Cross over the road, bearing slightly east. You are now going to follow Akeman Street for 6 miles, as it runs, practically straight, to Old Whitehill Farm, near Tackley. For much of its length Akeman Street acts as a parish boundary, and here it divides Combe from Stonesfield. The path enters a small copse and then runs north-east along the field boundary, climbing gradually out of the Evenlode valley until the hedge ends and the remains of a stone wall take over. Follow the field boundary. Beyond the end of this field you

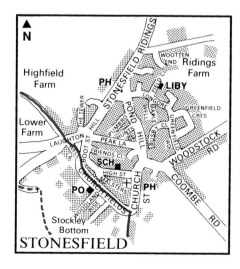

STONESFIELD

36

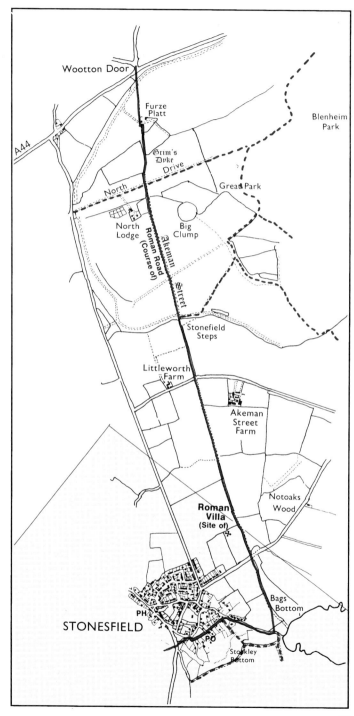

37

will come to a small patch of scrubland with three small elm trees. You may be treading on human bones here, for, according to the rector's book recording the perambulation of Stonesfield parish in 1807 the spot is known as Allen's Grave. To the people of Wootton, however, according to the Wootton parish enclosure award of 1770, it is called Holland's Grave. We know nothing today of Allen or Holland, or even whether in fact they were one and the same person, but they are buried in a place with a great windswept view. Stand and look west to Stonesfield village and the Evenlode valley, south to Combe village, and north to Kingswood and Wootton Wood. The fields are large and open, with a few hedges and trees, and the sky seems vast, almost as if one were in East Anglia. The landscape will be very different a mile further on in the sheltered confines of Blenheim Park.

From Allen's or Holland's Grave Akeman Street follows the western side of the hedge boundary for the length of two fields until it reaches the Littleworth/Combe road. You can clearly see the foundations of the Roman road here, with a substantial drop into the lower-lying fields of Combe, and there are several old trees bordering it. Cross over the Littleworth/Combe road, and continue on to Stonesfield Steps, a wooden ladder-stile set in Blenheim Park Wall. You can clearly see the blocked-up entrance gate in the wall, for this ancient route is far more than a public footpath. It was for centuries one of the principal highways across England, and was described in the Wootton enclosure award of 1770 as 'Akeman Street Road'. Akeman Street is now going to take you straight across Blenheim Park. From Stonesfield Steps the path goes straight down through a belt of trees and bushes to reach a woodland ride. The next section is a little difficult, bearing east-north-east through the copse to the edge of a huge field. Ahead of you across the field lie two clumps of trees. First look for the 'Big Clump'; then, and further north again, a small neat clump of lime trees, which at certain times of the year appear from a distance to be completely leafed in red. From here Akeman Street is clearly defined above the level of the field.

Having reached the cart-track going east, continue past the little clump of limes, and North Lodge, both on your left, to a field-gate. Passing through the gate you cross over Grim's Dyke to the North Drive, the great mile-long, tree-lined drive which forms the grand vista to Blenheim Palace seen on your right, and continue north-east along a good cart-track with the earthworks of Grim's Dyke plainly visible on your right, and proceed down a gentle slope to a field-gate. Grim was a by-name of the heathen god Woden. The Anglo-Saxons often attributed to him the building of the prehistoric earthworks they encountered, hence the frequent occurrence in different parts of the country of Grim's

Dyke or Ditches. At the bottom of the slope go through a gate, then climb up to a farm cottage, known as Furze Platt. From here continue east-north-east across the field to a belt of trees, and left through the trees to the huge Wootton Door set in Blenheim Park Wall.

Wootton Door (A44) to Kirtlington

Open Wootton Door and almost like Alice in Wonderland, step into a different world. A short wide track leads to the A44.

Take the road forking right just after crossing the A44. This is one of the metalled stretches of Akeman Street and is straight and narrow. It is called Stratford Lane. Keep a keen eye and ear open for fast motor traffic. Before dropping down to the Glyme valley stop and look at the view. You have been travelling for many miles along the lovely Evenlode valley, gradually climbing out of that valley from Stonesfield Ford, and passing through the trim enclosed parkland of Blenheim Palace. Now you can see two new river valleys which flow into the Evenlode, right over into the valley of the Cherwell. From the ancient Roman road you can now see some very prominent modern features, the large white chimney of Shipton-on-Cherwell cement works, the radio mast at Beckley on the Oxford Heights, and the great bulk of the John Radcliffe hospital at Headington.

Carry on down Stratford Lane to Stratford Bridge over the Glyme, then straight on uphill to Sansom's Farm and cottages. Here you cross the B4027 and continue straight on along the cart-track on the far side.

You are still on Akeman Street, that stands clear above the fields on either side until it reaches the crossroads with Dornford Lane. This is an ancient green lane, coming into existence around 1100 for the purpose of carrying supplies from the royal demesne farm at Steeple Barton to the royal manor of Woodstock. It is very different from Akeman Street, for it follows the valley as much as it can, curves when it suits it, and is bounded by high and ancient hedges. You, however, crossing Dornford Lane, continue your straight and austere route, north-easterly uphill, still along a very good wide grass track. Eventually you come to another crossing with a green lane, Slough Lane. This little green crossroads is a good sheltered spot for a rest and a snack. If the winds are blowing hard a better one will not be found on the eastern side of the A423 until you are well down into the Cherwell valley.

From the crossroads Akeman Street continues straight on, but has become narrow. It emerges on to the A423 just north of Strudy's Castle Inn.

Stonesfield: a gloving factory, 1959

Cross over the A423 with great care. It is now a thoroughly busy modern road, but is as ancient as the Ridgeway, a prehistoric route using the ridge between the Cherwell valley and the valleys whose rivers flow into the Evenlode. Take the Tackley road and continue along Akeman Street which goes off through a stile and gate on your right. Akeman Street continues downhill, first between banks and hedges, then through fields to reach the Whitehill road. All the way down you can enjoy good views of the Chilterns and Brill and Muswell Hills; also of Kirtlington, the next village on the Oxfordshire Way. Cross the road and carry straight on with Tackley Park Wall on your left. After climbing five stiles you cross a plank bridge over a little stream.

Here at last you leave Akeman Street and, bearing right, take a well-used track across a field, to a stile and gate on to a lane by the east side of Field Cottage, Old Whitehill. Look around and you will see in the pasture fields the unmistakable signs of the site of old Whitehill village, deserted long ago – but why and when no-one knows.

Continuing on to Kirtlington go east along the lane, passing the sewage works on your right, and continuing along a grass cart-track

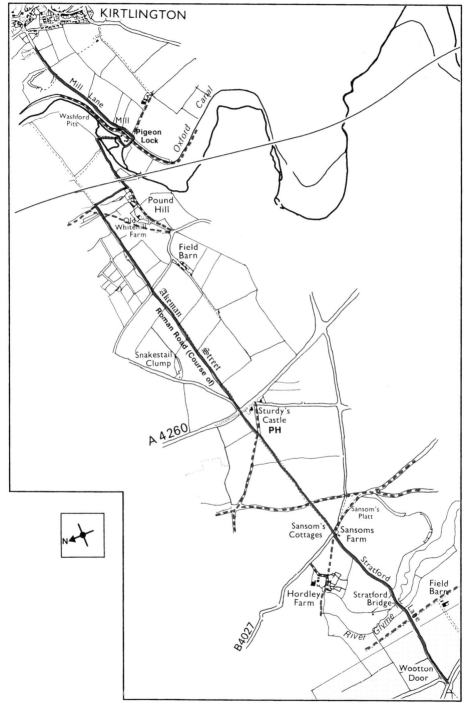

KIRTLINGTON

Mill Lane

Washford Pits

Mill

Oxford Canal

Pigeon Lock

Pound Hill

Old Whitehill Farm

Field Barn

Akeman Street

Roman Road (Course of)

Snakestail Clump

Sturdy's Castle PH

A 4260

N

Sansom's Platt

Sansom's Cottages

Sansoms Farm

Stratford

Hordley Farm

Stratford Bridge

Glyme Lane

Field Barn

B4027

River Glyme

Wootton Door

41

Stonesfield

above the Cherwell, which here offers a good bathing place.

The bridleway continues to a good metal bridlegate leading to a concrete bridge over a branch of the River Cherwell. From a small grass island you cross another concrete bridge over a second branch of the Cherwell. A well-used track leads across a grass field to a stile for walkers or a bridlegate for riders, leading straight down to the ford, where the Cherwell flows over the original main street. The house on your left is Flight's Mill. The Oxfordshire Way here leaves the district of West Oxfordshire which it first entered at Foscot on the Gloucestershire boundary, and now enters Cherwell District. You have finally left behind the furthermost part of the dip slope of the Cotswolds. A new world lies beyond – clay country, intermingled with the Corallian limestone of the Oxford Heights.

If you are feeling adventurous, and would like to cool your feet, you can essay the ford; otherwise use the weir and foot-bridges and walk behind Flight's Mill to the meadow beyond. Flight's Mill is now a private residence, and appears to have acquired its name in 1692. There is evidence of two thirteenth-century mills on opposite sides of the river. Turn east at the meadow, and you will arrive at the Oxford Canal, completed in 1790. Cross at the lock and continue up a long lane past the stone quarry (Washford Pits) to the north, and into the village of Kirtlington.

Stonesfield

Stonesfield is a most interesting village, stone-built, climbing up a hill, very confusing to the wayfarer with its many streets. The church, Early English, suffered what Pevsner refers to as 'lunatic restoration' when in 1876 a new north aisle was built, completely destroying its small scale. There is some interesting armorial glass.

Everyone who knows Oxfordshire must know and love the stone roof tiles which add so much beauty to the villages and towns, and indeed to many of the Oxford colleges. Not everyone will know that these are known as Stonesfield slates, because they all came from the parish of Stonesfield. The mining of these stone slates stopped early in this century, and they can now only be obtained at great expense, and with a degree of good luck, when an old house or barn is demolished.

You can still see a few signs of the old quarrying operations. Most of the many small quarries were worked by only two or three local men. The 'mines' were either in the side of a steep valley or holes in the ground, rather like large wells, perhaps 60 feet deep, with galleries leading off them. Large stone slabs were brought to the surface and left there to weather. In due course the frost split them into thin layers, after which they were fixed to battens in the roof. It is no wonder that, after so natural and patient a method of manufacture, the true Stonesfield slate roof is so beautiful and so subtle in its colouring.

The village is well known to geologists for the remarkable fossils found in the neighbourhood. There is a fine Georgian manor house, with a large garden occasionally open to the public.

Kirtlington to Weston-on-the-Green

Leave Kirtlington by turning south in the main street just past the stone-built modern primary school, and then bear east to the entrance of Kirtlington Park. This elegant Palladian mansion was built between 1742 and 1746 for Sir James Dashwood. It is in private ownership and no footpath goes close enough for the house to be seen, but a distant view of the south front can be glimpsed if you look back after leaving the village. The footpath takes you east across the park (laid out by Capability Brown between 1755 and 1762) and north of the fishponds to a belt of trees called the Long Plantation. Continue east through this plantation. Your path continues east across one more field to an old lane, crosses the lane and one more field, then veers south-east to a foot-bridge.

Continue south-east through a pasture that clearly reveals its ridge-and-furrow past. At the end of this field continue on this footpath, to the east of a bungalow, to come out by the church.

Kirtlington

This is a pleasant stone-built village on the A4095. It has existed since Saxon times, and its church dates from the twelfth and thirteenth centuries.

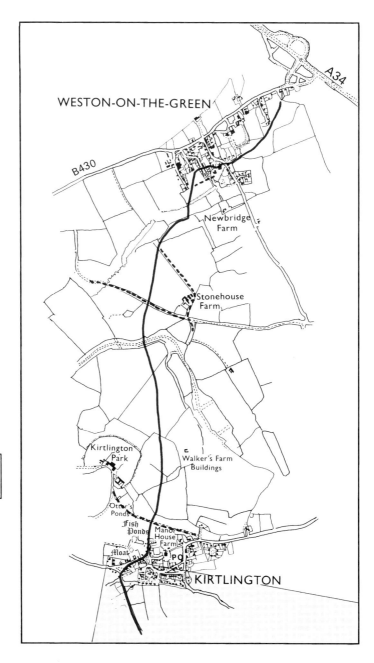

Weston-on-the-Green to Islip

3½ MILES

5½ KILOMETRES

CUMULATIVE

33 ½ MILES
54 ½ KILOMETRES

Leave Weston-on-the-Green by crossing the road immediately south of the church, and take the track opposite, through a kissing gate, until you reach a foot-bridge on the left over a stream. Turning immediately right follow the left edge of the field, which runs beside Weston-on-the-Green Manor grounds. Cross the foot-bridge in the hedge and walk across the field diagonally to a hedged corner by a tennis court. Maintain your route to a gateway near some farm buildings. Carry straight on to a stile in the railings of the pub car-park. Proceed to the car-park entrance and turn left to the mini roundabout. Follow the metalled footpath over the road-bridge crossing the A34. At the top of the bridge cross over and follow the grass verge to the minor road junction. Turn right and right again to a metalled farm access track. When it starts to run through the second large field look out for a footpath on the right which leads you straight to a foot-bridge. Carry on across a meadow and head towards the right of two stiles in the fence. Go straight on to a foot-bridge, then cut across the next meadow to a kink in the right side of the field. Continue straight on towards the right field corner where there is a stile. Follow the hedgeline to another stile and foot-bridge. At the metalled farm access turn right for a short distance, then left on to a track. Turn left off the track through a gateway, then right to follow the ditched hedgeline to the stile. Cross over and use the path which runs through the small copse. Once over the white stile take extreme care of oncoming trains, and turn right for about 50 yards before crossing the Bicester/Oxford railway line to another white stile and ramp. Head towards the right side of the field by cutting the corner to the foot-bridge and stile. Go straight across the field to the far left corner and through the gateway. Turn left over a stile and head diagonally to the field corner; then bear right and over a stile into North Street, Islip.

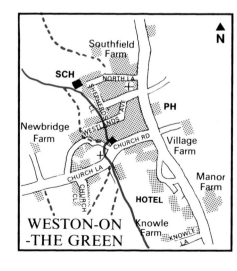

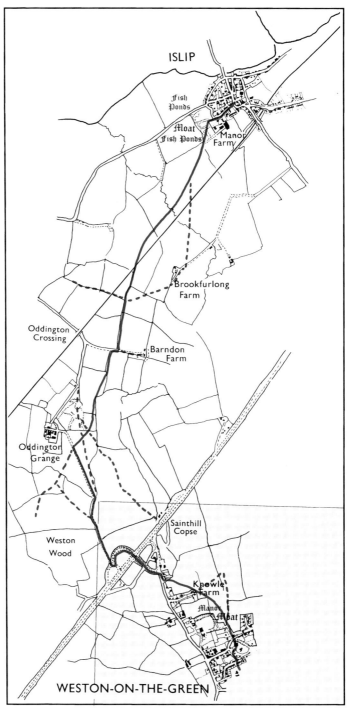

Weston-on-the-Green Manor: an aerial view

Weston-on-the-Green

Weston-on-the-Green is now a village of mixed architectural styles and periods. There are several pleasant stone-built and thatched cottages, and the stocks still stand on the green, most of which has now disappeared. The church is worth a visit, especially to see the splendid doorcases, unexpectedly grand for a little village church. The tub-shaped font is Norman, and the altarpiece is a painting attributed to Pompeo Batoni. The most interesting building in the village is Weston Manor, now a hotel. This was originally a medieval building, belonging to the bailiffs of Osney Abbey, and was remodelled about 1540 by Lord Williams of Thame, whom we shall meet again as the builder of Beckley Park. The present façade was built c. 1820, and during the nineteenth century a good deal of the interior was remodelled.

A horse-drawn reaper, 1900

Islip to Beckley

Passing through Noke

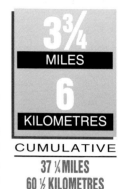

Leaving Islip, cross the bridge over the Ray on the south side of the village and continue along the road up a steep hill, until you come to an allotment entrance on your left. Turn in here unless it is a sunny day, when it is well worth your while to walk a little further up the road to enjoy the delightful view of Islip village with the sun picking out the gilding on the church tower. The footpath goes past the allotment, and continues south-east through several fields almost parallel to the B4027. Immediately to the east you get your first fine view across Otmoor, and on a clear day you can see the parish churches of the Otmoor 'towns' ringing the moor. To the north-east can be seen Graven Hill outside Bicester, and the TV and radio transmitter at Beckley. The footpath takes you to the road that runs down from the B4027 to the village of Noke.

Follow the road right through the village until you come nearly to the end of the road in Lower Noke and join the bridleway. This follows the edge of a large field. There is a wide grass verge with the hedge on the right (western side), gradually rising south-easterly for about half a mile. On reaching the remains of a triangular copse continue to the edge of Noke Wood. When you reach the wood continue along the field boundary for 500 yards, turn right and go straight on through it, entering South Oxfordshire. Cross one small field over a ditch and stile and climb south-east up a steep field to a field-gate leading into Church Lane. Just before entering Beckley pause to look back at a fine view over Otmoor to the north (you have climbed 150 feet from Noke Wood into Beckley). Then walk up Church Lane into the main street of the village.

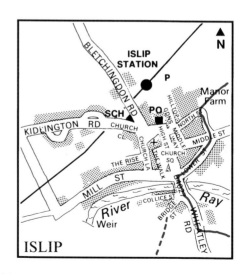

Islip

Islip is a beautiful, well-preserved village standing near the confluence of the rivers Ray and Cherwell. There are many pleasing buildings, notably the Old Rectory, built in

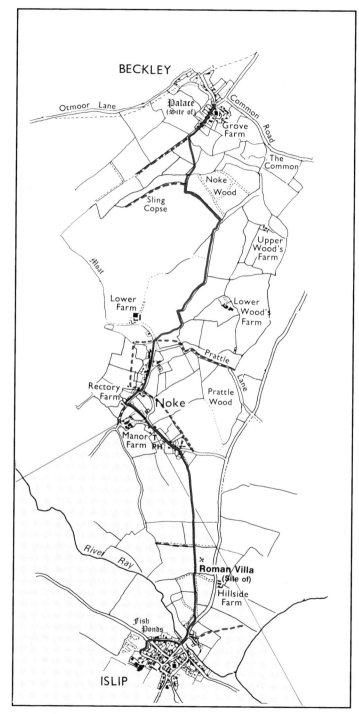

1690 by the Rector, Dr South, who also founded and endowed the village school in 1710. Other buildings to note are Manor Farm in Upper Street (sixteenth century) and a house in High Street (seventeenth century) formerly the King's Head Inn. Islip lay on the coach route from London to Worcester and had at one time twenty-one inns. Now there are but two: the Red Lion and the Swan Inn. While refreshing yourself at one of these you may contemplate the ancient fame of Islip and its place in English history. In the last field you crossed before entering the village once stood a palace of Ethelred the Unready, where in AD 1004 King Edward the Confessor was born. When King Edward built Westminster Abbey he gave to it the manor of Islip. Islip provided two great ecclesiastics in the middle ages, Simon of Islip who became Archbishop of Canterbury in 1348, and John of Islip who became Prior of Westminster in 1500 and thus presided over the building of the Henry VII chapel.

As befits a village with such a history, Islip church dominates the scene. Its beautiful three-storey tower was built in the fifteenth century. There is almost as much history, however, in the bridge over the River Ray at the southern end of the village. In the Civil War Islip was an important outpost in the Royalist defence of their headquarters at Oxford, and in 1645 Cromwell defeated the Royalist forces in a skirmish at Islip Bridge. The old stone bridge with its four arches was rebuilt in 1878. Until the latter part of the nineteenth century, when drainage and new cuttings partially tamed the River Ray, reducing its size and propensity to flood, Islip was a prime source for fish supplies. Besides coarse fish, eels and crayfish were plentiful, wildfowl were to be had in season, and osier reeds were cut from the river banks.

Noke

'I went to Noke and nobody spoke; I went to Beckley and they spoke directly; They said at Bicester "well, ow be mister?".'

So goes the old doggerel, but as the Oxfordshire Way does not go through Bicester you will have to find out the full truth of it on some other occasion.

Noke is a tiny village, almost unspoilt by modern development, though there are some new little houses and bungalows, mostly in Lower Noke. The name is derived from 'the oak tree', recalling the origin of the village as a clearway in the forest on the edge of the fen. There are still a few oak trees surviving from the large oak forests of the past. The church is tiny, dating from the early thirteenth century, and restored in 1883. When Edward the Confessor granted the fees of

Islip Hall from the bridge,
c. 1930

Islip to the Abbey of Westminster part of the parish of Noke was included in the grant. Those who paid tithes to Islip buried their dead in Islip churchyard, and to this day the path from Islip to Noke is known as the 'Wake' or 'Coffin' path.

The Manor Farm is a fine building with work from the late sixteenth to the eighteenth centuries, and the Old Rectory has a central block dating from the seventeenth century with eighteenth- and nineteenth-century extensions. It is noteworthy that with these extensions the Rectory is now considerably larger than the church itself. The Plough Inn was originally a cottage and probably dates from the seventeenth century.

53

Beckley to Waterperry

Passing near Horton-cum-Studley

Walking eastward through Beckley village you climb up a shady lane and through a gate on to an open farm track. To the north you look over eastern Otmoor to the Buckinghamshire hills beyond. After about 200 yards leave the track by a stile on your left, and cross two fields, the third field drops down steeply to a copse, and as you descend you will see to your left the moated Lower Park Farm, or Beckley Park. At the bottom of the slope a stile leads on to a little woodland path running along the left bank of a stream. Just before emerging on to the road, which is the private drive to Beckley Park, you cross this stream by a plank bridge. Go diagonally across the next field via a stile in a fence midway to a gate at the eastern corner, continue across a rather boggy field to a gateway with an accommodation bridge, then straight on to a stile. You should follow the right-hand side of the hedge until it begins to curve away on your left. You veer right here, and cross the rest of the field to a stile leading on to a farm drive a few yards from the Woodperry, Horton-cum-Studley road. Ever since crossing Beckley Park drive you have been walking over the level, often boggy, fields of Otmoor. On the hill ahead of you can be seen Studley Priory.

Cross straight over the road and through a gate opposite on to a bridleway which skirts Studley Wood on the left and then, when the wood bears off to the left, carries straight on across a field to a bridle-bridge and gate. Go straight across the next field to reach a green lane.

Across the green lane the path continues between fences, skirts Stanton Little Wood on the east and south sides, then bears off left to a T-junction. Turn left here, following the left bank of a stream and skirting the left-hand side of the buildings of Danesbrook (formerly Menmarsh) Farm. Beyond the farmyard the bridleway follows the metalled farmhouse drive to Menmarsh Guide Post, the junction of three roads. One of these roads leads to the stone-built village of Stanton St John, a place of pilgrimage for Americans as a house

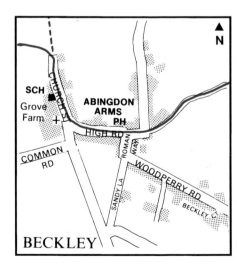

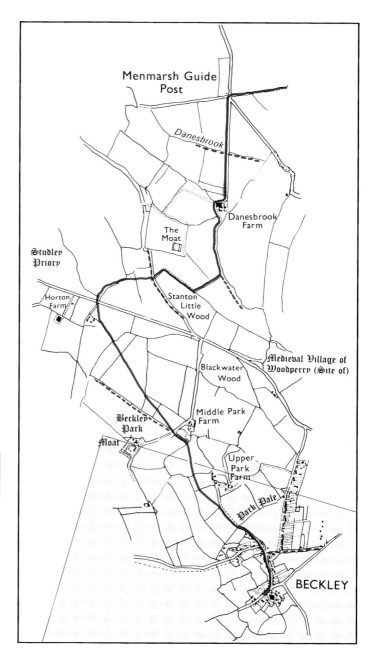

Beckley: cottages from the churchyard

opposite the church is the birthplace of John White, founder of the state of Massachusetts. Follow the bridleway which goes south as a wide track between a hedge and a fence. At the end you come to two gates, turn left through the first, right through the second, and enter a long field with Moorbirge Brook on your right and Bernwood Forest on your left. The bridleway at first follows the brook, then, as the brook curves away to the right, carries on round the edge of the Bernwood Forest, past Polecat End to Drunkard's Corner. At Drunkard's Corner you come to a gate leading into a hedged lane. Do not go through this gate, but turn right, just before reaching it and make for a conspicuous foot-bridge. Do not cross this bridge either, but instead turn left, crossing two foot-bridges and following the hedge; then cross a road and continue until you have just passed Park Farm on your left. The path now carries on south for half a mile to join a metalled road. Continue for nearly a mile down this road, crossing a staggered cross-roads near Townsend Farm, until you come to Waterperry village.

Beckley

Beckley is a delightful stone village standing on a ridge of the Oxford Heights 350 feet above the 4 square mile plain of Otmoor. Round this

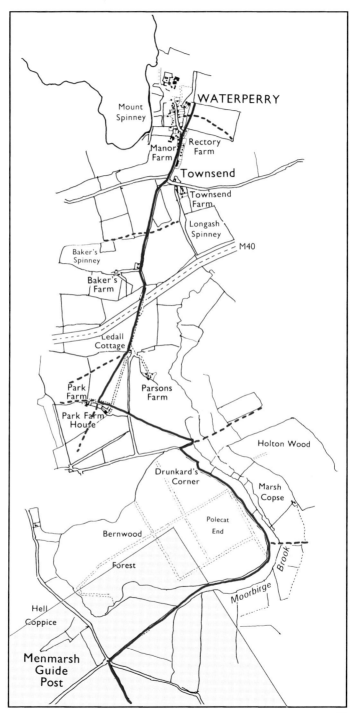

N

plain stand the seven Otmoor 'towns', Beckley, Noke, Horton, Oddington, Fencott, Murcott and Charlton-on-Otmoor.

At the time of the Norman Conquest Beckley was the largest of these settlements. William the Conqueror gave the manor of Beckley to Robert D'Oilly. His descendants, the name now spelt Deeley, still hold property locally. Nothing remains of the former palace of Beckley, nor of the deer park enclosed in 1197, but there are many charming old houses in Beckley.

The church of St Mary was originally Norman, rebuilt in the fourteenth and fifteenth centuries. There is some early stained glass, wall paintings and a Jacobean pulpit.

When you leave the village and plunge down towards the moor you will be fortunate to see, to the north-east, a beautiful old house, standing quiet and alone amid peaceful fields. This is Beckley Park, built around 1540 by Lord Williams of Thame, possibly as a hunting lodge. The history of the site, and of the three moats, goes back many centuries before that. King Alfred once owned it and perhaps the triple moats date from the ninth century. Robert D'Oilly sold it in 1227 to Richard Earl of Cornwall, who built his hunting lodge there. Lord Williams of Thame built the present house between the outer and middle moats. It is a simple, unpretentious house of deep red brick with stone mullioned windows, and it stands amid its fields in perfect peace. It is a Grade 1 listed building.

In Beckley village one is always conscious of Otmoor. A Roman road from Dorchester to Alchester (a fort near Bicester) passed through Beckley and crossed the moor from south to north. You can still cross Otmoor as the Romans did; the road is now called Otmoor Lane.

Otmoor means 'Otta's fen'. The bed of Otmoor contains a layer of Oxford clay, and for centuries Otmoor has been a swamp ringed by rough pasture. This was common land for the villages round the edge, and from the swamps and river they could take wildfowl and fish. This way of life persisted for centuries, until the moor was forcibly enclosed in 1830. The Otmoor Riots that enclosure provoked are famous, and the Otmoor men battled for many years against this loss of their ancient common rights. But 'progress' won in the end, the River Ray was re-channelled, and new drains dug, though these measures were never wholly successful in draining the moor. It remained a lonely, wild place, a haven for birds and plants. Up till a few years ago the view from Beckley, especially at sunset, presented a strange picture of little fields

Beckley church

*covered by grass, rushes and sedge of many different colours.
Some say that Lewis Carroll had the idea of Alice's chess-board in*
Through the Looking Glass *after looking down on Otmoor from
Beckley.*

Waterperry to Rycote

Passing through Waterstock, Tiddington and Albury

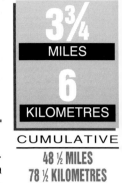
After passing the first few houses in Waterperry the road bends left. Here you keep straight on through a gate and follow the bridleway with glimpses of the village to your left, and good views of Waterperry House. Beyond the house turn left down a well-used narrow path to join the drive of Waterperry House as it emerges through its gates. Follow the fenced drive which crosses the River Thame by a brick arch known as Bow Bridge.

The path passes the delightful Mill House and crosses a paddock to join the village road. Turn left past the church and you will soon come to a gate on your right. Turn in here and strike across the meadow to a stile hidden in a fold of the ground, just south of Home Farm. Continue straight on following the obvious waymarked path, with a right-angle bend, over the golf course (built in 1993) until it brings you out on to the A418.

Turn left along the road for 100 yards, then take a path on the right which crosses the disused railway track and then goes diagonally across two fields to a small foot-bridge. It then climbs past an idyllic thatched cottage, turns left beyond the cottage garden then right over a stile, crossing a field to reach the sunken Sandy Lane. It goes nearly straight across (very slightly to the left) and, for you are now in hilly country, drops down to the village road between some modern houses.

On reaching Tiddington cross over the road and take the path opposite, which, starting as an access road to some houses, goes through a wicket gate and down a field to a small foot-bridge. It then climbs through another field to arrive at Albury. A wicket gate leads on to a road and you then go through the gate of Church Farm. The path becomes a broad gated track with good views to the left over the River Thame to Shabbington in Buckinghamshire. On reaching the farm follow the track round to

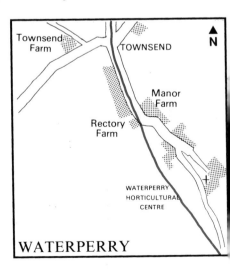

WATERPERRY

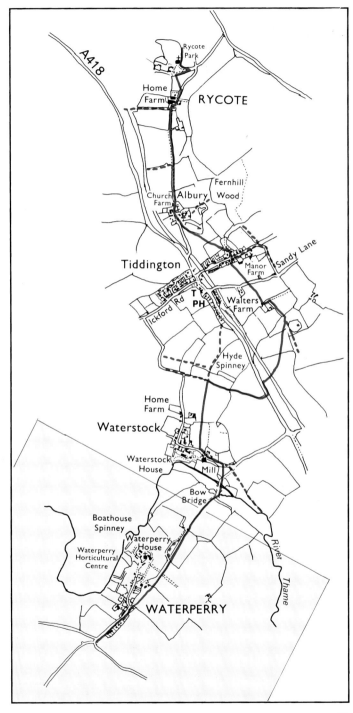

A418

Rycote
Park

Home
Farm

RYCOTE

Fernhill
Wood

Church
Farm

Albury

Tiddington

Manor
Farm

Sandy Lane

Ickford Rd

T
PH

Walters
Farm

Hyde
Spinney

Home
Farm

Waterstock

Waterstock
House

Mill

Bow
Bridge

Boathouse
Spinney

Waterperry
House

Waterperry
Horticultural
Centre

River Thame

WATERPERRY

N

the right, passing on the right of most of the buildings and the farmhouse. Just past the farmhouse turn left through a gate, and cross the field diagonally to a stile leading to another driveway and your first sight of Rycote Park and chapel.

Waterperry

This tiny village has a most interesting and delightful little church, with a surviving Saxon arch and an unusual wooden tower. The eighteenth-century box pews still have their original brass candlesticks, and there is a seventeenth-century three-decker pulpit. There is some good glass, armorial bearings and monuments, and several brasses, including the curious palimpsest Curson Brass.

Waterperry House retains a seventeenth-century wing, though most of the house was remodelled in the eighteenth century. Part of the gardens now form the Waterperry Horticultural Centre, offering day courses for gardeners, and shrubs and plants for sale to the public.

Tiddington

This small village lies astride a crossroads, and is a mixture of old and modern housing, the latter now predominating. The church, isolated above the main settlement of Tiddington, is in the tiny hamlet of Albury on its hill. It is a nineteenth-century building on an ancient site.

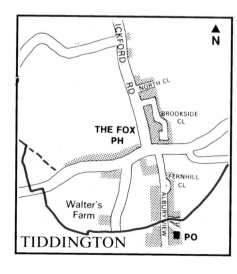

Waterperry House in the 1930s

Ploughing, c. 1915

Rycote to Tetsworth

The Oxfordshire Way turns right on to this driveway and after a few yards at a junction turns sharp left on to another driveway. By Rycote chapel turn right on to the chapel path, passing to the right of the chapel, and entering a wood. Follow an obvious waymarked path through the wood, bearing right at one point where you gain a glimpse of Rycote House to your left, and you will reach a wooden gate into fields. A small lake can just be glimpsed on the left. Carry straight on across the fields to a stile at the edge of Old Paddock Wood. The path through the wood first bends left, then curves back to the right. It is very easy to lose your way, so follow the waymarks, being particularly careful to bear left at one fork. A final rather boggy section will bring you out on to the A329 road.

Cross the A329 and on to the Oxfordshire Golf Course. Follow the path, keeping well to the right of the Club House, and over Lobbersdown Hill take in the extensive views across the course. The path goes through a gap in the hedge near a pond and runs down the left-hand side of the hedge to a small gate. Follow the right-hand hedge downhill for half a mile through three fields, ignoring a gate and foot-bridge to the right. At the bottom end of the third field go straight on over a foot-bridge; then turn left and follow the stream on your right. The path passes between the stream and sewage treatment works, then keeping along the left-hand side of the hedge passes Spencers (formerly Home) Farm at the top of the field on the left. Soon after this it reaches a stile on to the concrete farm road. Turn right here, and cross the big village green to the A40 road.

Rycote

Rycote is one of the most remote and fascinating settlements lying along the Oxfordshire Way, and you must not fail to spare a few minutes to visit the chapel, restored and maintained by the Department of the Environment, which opened it to the public in 1967. Built by Sir Richard Quatremains of Rycote and his wife Sybil, it was consecrated in 1449. Henry VIII, Elizabeth I, James I and Charles I were all visitors at Rycote Park and worshipped in the chapel, which no doubt accounts for the splendour of the royal pew. It was probably built for Queen .Elizabeth but, impressive as it is, it is only one of the many glories of Rycote chapel.

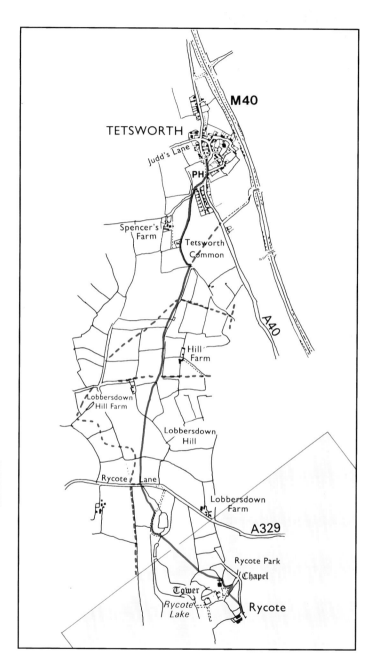

Rycote Park: the ruined turret, c. 1904

Rycote chapel

    Rycote Park fits peacefully into its deeply rural setting. A great house, red brick with blue diaper design, moated and built round a courtyard, stood here in the sixteenth century, but the greater part of this was burned down in 1745. The ruins were finally cleared from the site in 1800, only a turret and some stable buildings surviving, and these were converted into the present house around 1920.

Tetsworth to Pyrton

Passing through Adwell and
Wheatfield

5
MILES

8
KILOMETRES

CUMULATIVE
56 ¼ MILES
91 KILOMETRES

In Tetsworth cross the A40 and go up a road called Parkers Hill. On the left you will see an old cobbled pathway serving as a raised pavement. This leads directly through a kissing gate. Cross a small field to a stile. There is a fine view of the Chilterns ahead, with the Berkshire Downs to the right. Now go down the next, larger, field and, passing directly under the M40 motorway, you will soon come to a gate and stile leading on to Harlesford Lane.

Go straight over the stone stile, then bear left across a field to a stile. Now maintain this direction across two further fields, passing through two gates and reaching a stile and foot-bridge in the far corner of the second field. On emerging on to the Tetsworth–Stoke Talmage road, bear half right across it to a gate virtually opposite, then cross a field diagonally to a stile. Maintain this direction across the next field to reach a foot-bridge under a willow tree. At the far end of the bridge turn left, crossing the corner of a field to a further foot-bridge. Cross this bridge and the fence at the far end of it, then continue straight on beside the left-hand stream until you reach a stile by a copse and ornamental lake to your left. Now continue straight on across a paddock to a stile into a wood, then go straight on through this wood, with occasional glimpses on your left of the gardens of Adwell House. These are opened to the public once or twice a year. At the far side of the wood go through a gate into a narrow paddock, then walk the length of the paddock to a gate and stile on to the road into Adwell.

Turn right along the tree-lined road and follow it with parkland to your right for a third of a mile. Among the parkland and roadside trees you will discover the now rare sight of live elm trees, some of the few remaining examples of what must originally have been the county's most profuse hedgerow tree before the ravages of Dutch elm disease in the

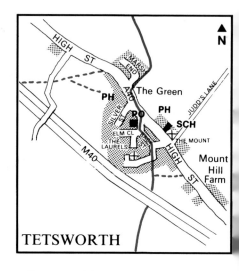

TETSWORTH

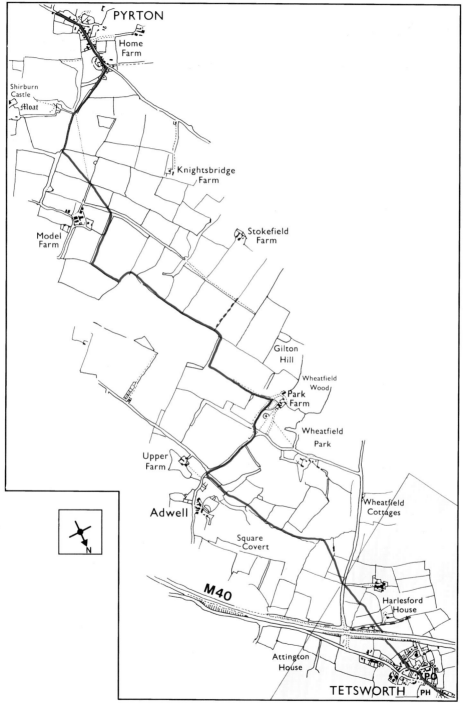

mid-1970s. On reaching a sharp right-hand bend turn left on to a private road, and follow it to Wheatfield Park on your right, past the tiny parish church. Taking the left-hand turning at a fork, continue until you come level with Park Farm to your right.

Near Park Farm turn left up a fenced track, which leads you over the brow of the hill, with fine views of the Chilterns ahead, into an arable field. Now follow a fence straight on downhill until you reach a crossing hedge, then turn right and follow the hedge to the far side of the field. Here cross a stile and foot-bridge and turn left. You are now in Lord Macclesfield's Shirburn estate. Follow the left-hand hedge downhill through three fields to a foot-bridge over a brook, along the edge of a left-hand copse through three fields, and gradually swing left to reach a stile. Do not cross this stile, but instead turn right beside the left-hand hedge uphill to the top left-hand corner of the field; then turn right and follow the top hedge until you reach a track through it towards Model Farm. This farm, which was built by an earlier Lord Macclesfield in 1857, was so called as when it was built it was one of the most technologically advanced farms in the country. Although it resembles one of Blake's 'satanic mills' it is therefore of considerable historical interest as an early example of the mechanization which has revolutionized modern agriculture.

Here transfer to the other side of the hedge and resume your previous direction until you reach another crossing farm road. Cross this farm road, then bear half left, crossing two fields diagonally to reach double-gates, just right of a cottage, which lead you on to the ancient Lower Icknield Way. Now turn right on to this ancient track, from which you may catch a glimpse of Shirburn Castle (built in 1377) through the trees to your left, and follow its hedged course for half a mile to reach Pyrton village by one of the castle lodges opposite the Plough Inn.

Tetsworth

Tetsworth is quite a sizeable red-brick village, not quite large enough, perhaps, to merit such a huge village green. There are some very old and picturesque houses, including sixteen listed buildings, and a good deal of modern development, inevitable because of its proximity to Oxford and because it is traversed by the A40 which, until the construction of the adjacent M40 motorway, carried a tremendous load of traffic between London and Oxford. Tetsworth is now effectively bypassed by the M40. The Swan Hotel is a fine Elizabethan coaching inn, remodelled about 1700, and faced with red and blue chequered bricks. The chimneys at the back are the originals.

Tetsworth: Swan Hill, c. 1906

Adwell

The tiny village of Adwell has never been much larger, but it has dwindled in recent years. Adwell House, which was rebuilt in the late eighteenth century, is noted for its Grecian staircase. The nearby parish church was rebuilt in 1865 by Arthur Blomfield, when it proved impossible to repair the original twelfth-century building due to structural weakness, but vestiges of the old church were retained in the new structure. In addition, the village boasts several seventeenth-century cottages and since the construction of the M40 in 1972–4 it has become even more remote, as the extension of the village street to the A40 was severed by the motorway.

Wheatfield

Today it is barely possible to say there is a 'village' of Wheatfield, as the twenty-eight inhabitants of the parish counted in 1981 are scattered across its 740 acres in isolated farms and groups of cottages, and its church in the middle of parkland is the only physical sign of its existence. Up until the eighteenth century, however, the medieval church, which was completely remodelled at this time, stood in a street of old cottages, traces of the foundations of which can still be clearly seen in Wheatfield Park. When Wheatfield Park House was rebuilt by John Rudge, to the west of the church, the cottages were felt to spoil the appearance of the park and so they were demolished, their inhabitants being rehoused elsewhere. Today all that remains are the stable block and other outbuildings which now form Park Farm, as the house itself was totally destroyed by fire on New Year's Day 1814, but its terraced foundations can still be seen between the church and the farm.

Pyrton to Christmas Common

2¼ MILES

3½ KILOMETRES

CUMULATIVE
58 ½ MILES
94 ½ KILOMETRES

From the Plough Inn follow the road south to St Mary's church and the entrance to Pyrton Manor on your right, continuing along the roadside footway until you reach the B4009, Thame to Watlington, road. Go straight across and continue past the site of the old Watlington railway station to Pyrton Field Farm. Here the metalled roadway becomes a gravelled track. Within half a mile you will be crossing the hedge-lined Icknield Way. This ancient trackway here forms part of the Ridgeway National Trail and if you chose to leave the Oxfordshire Way here you could follow the Ridgeway as far as the neolithic stone circles of Avebury, to the south-west, or to Ivinghoe Beacon, site of an early hilltop fort, to the north-east.

Cross the Icknield Way and climb up Pyrton Hill on to the Chiltern escarpment. You are now encountering the last major change of terrain in the county, entering on to the chalk uplands of the Chilterns. The contrast with the rest of Oxfordshire is startling – hanging beechwoods and bluebells, flint churches and cottages roofed with thatch or clay tiles – and it is difficult to remember that only a short while back you were walking over the Cotswold limestones or dropping down into the Gault Clay vale. Here there is gorse, practically never seen on the Cotswolds, and here, before entering the timbered area near the top, pause and look back at the splendid view over the vale of Oxford. As you pass into the tree-lined path look out for the footpath leading off to the right. Here you leave the bridleway, climb the stile in the corner of the paddock, cross it diagonally to the right and follow the field boundary up the hill until you reach the stile leading on to Christmas Common road. Turn right along this road past the junction with the Watlington road, and as far as the next fork. Take the right-hand road here, signposted Nettlebed and Henley, passing the telephone kiosk on your left and the Fox and Hounds on your right. About 50 yards past the pub the Oxfordshire Way leaves the road, to the left and over a green lawn between a row of cottages and the small church.

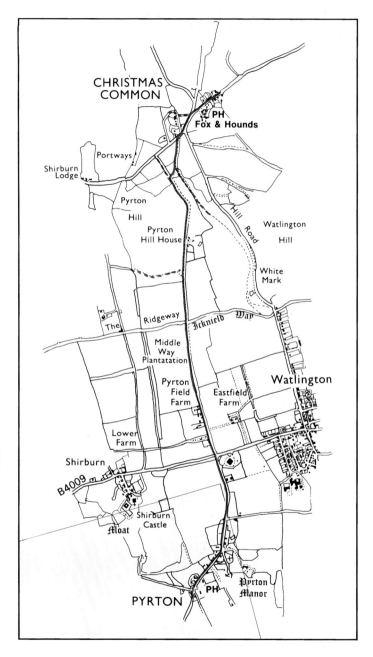

Pyrton Manor, c. 1904

Threshing, c. 1915

Pyrton

This is a tiny remote village of some fifty houses, mostly brick and flint with a little stone and some thatched roofs. It has wonderful snowdrops to delight those who walk early in the year. The seventeenth-century manor house, hidden within the park, was the home of Elizabeth Symeon, who was married to John Hampden in Pyrton church in 1619.

Christmas Common

Christmas Common itself is little more than a few scattered houses on the hilltop. There are no shops, and the church (a nineteenth-century building) has no special features. The Fox and Hounds is a pleasant brick and flint pub.

Christmas Common to Pishill

The footpath soon enters a thick wood, crosses another footpath, bears slightly left through conifers and emerges on to a narrow grit road beside a cottage called Glendarary. Turn right along this road past a farm entrance and into a wood. A sign tells you that it is part of Chiltern Forest. You will soon come to a path on your left which goes down through mature beech trees to the valley bottom. This bridleway follows the valley bottom, reaching patches of semi-mature trees and then a clearing. Here it bears left, and you leave it and turn right.

The footpath climbs up to the edge of the wood, then over a stile, and crosses a rising open field. From the top of the rise you can see a wooded corner with a farm in the background. Go towards the farm, passing two large ponds behind the trees, where you may well see wild duck. The farm is on Holland Ridge, which carries a rough road along it. Keeping to the north of the farm cross this by two stiles, and do not fail to pause to look at the view behind you.

After crossing the road follow the hedge and climb a stile into College Wood. Be careful not to take the right-hand branch which plunges down the steep slope of the valley, but keep high along the left edge of the beechwood, leaving it by a gate just as the path begins to drop down into another valley. Climb over a fence into a field, and follow the steep-sided valley until you reach the B480 just to the right of a converted farm. Cross the road, turn right and then immediately left up a little road to Pishill church. Follow this road until it turns right, where you go straight on through a gate.

Pishill

Pishill is a tiny place with a little church built in 1854 to replace a Norman building. There is some good Victorian glass and the south-west window of 1967 is by John Piper. There is an interesting thatched barn behind the rectory incorporating a thirteenth-century blocked window.

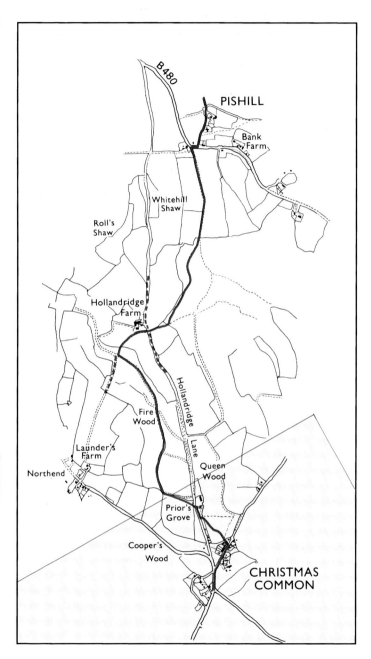

Pishill to Middle Assendon

4 MILES

6½ KILOMETRES

CUMULATIVE

65 ¼ MILES
105 ½ KILOMETRES

The bridleway follows the hedge across a meadow, dropping and rising to another mature beechwood. Go through a gate into the wood, cross another path and bear slightly right to climb the slope. Gain the ridge, where another footpath joins diagonally from the left. The two paths run together for a short distance and then one goes off to the right. You take the left fork, without losing height, and skirt a few trees to reach the Stonor road.

Cross the road and proceed squarely up the slope through more beechwoods to the top corner. Here go straight on. You are now in a crowned meadow; keep right and you will soon see Lodge Farm and cottage. A stile takes you over a fence on to a track between the buildings. There is a fine view from here.

Leaving Lodge Farm go straight on to Warmscombe Lane. This takes you down through dense woods which form part of the Warburg Trust belonging to the Berkshire, Buckinghamshire and Oxfordshire Naturalist Trust. This, with its mixed woods and devious valleys crossed by nature trails, is well worth a tour, and you are quite likely to see deer roaming through the woodlands.

Follow the bridleway until it curves left. Here continue straight on down a track having carefully avoided taking the much steeper track to the right.

There is a rough road at the bottom of the valley and you turn left along this. On the right, amid trees, is the ruin of St James, once the parish church of Bix when that hamlet was mainly down in the bottom. Continue along the road, which soon acquires a metalled surface and eventually reaches the B480 at Middle Assendon.

Middle Assendon

Middle Assendon, originally a small hamlet with no church, still has a few old houses and farms, but most of the development is modern.

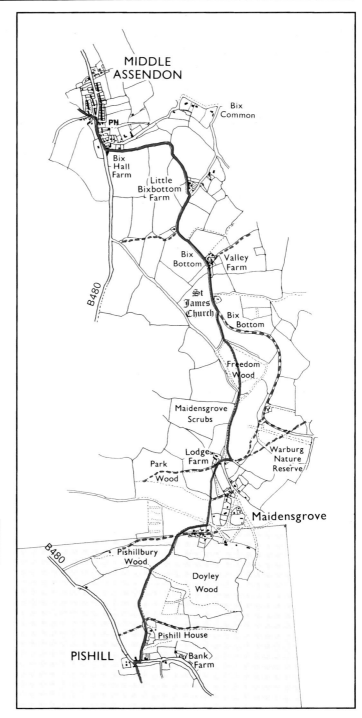

MIDDLE
ASSENDON

PH

Bix
Common

Bix
Hall
Farm

Little
Bixbottom
Farm

Bix
Bottom

Valley
Farm

B480

St
James
Church

Bix
Bottom

Freedom
Wood

Maidensgrove
Scrubs

Lodge
Farm

Park
Wood

Warburg
Nature
Reserve

Maidensgrove

N

B480

Pishillbury
Wood

Doyley
Wood

Pishill House

PISHILL

Bank
Farm

Middle Assendon to Henley-on-Thames

Go through the village to the Rainbow, cross the B480, cut through the trees, and take the road on the left of some houses; then go straight up the hill on a path. As you climb, another path goes off to the right, but ignore this, going instead into a meadow and climbing diagonally left, passing a corner hedge, straight up to the top. You might pause to get your breath and look back at the wide and impressive view behind you. As you reach the top, marked by a line of Scots pines, you will see a gap where the path goes through to another meadow. Here you cross the county boundary twice, but only for short distances, into Buckinghamshire. Continue diagonally right across this field, and over a stile in the hedge on to a road. This is close to a house with a pond in front of it. Cross the road and take the lane by the house. On your left is a hedge and line of mature trees; on your right the first of many fine trees, part of Henley Park. The road continues past fine oak, lime and beech trees. By a white house squeeze through a kissing gate to join another road coming in on the left. The road turns left near the clock-house of Henley Park, but you should go straight on through a kissing gate to a track. The track goes through open meadows along the ridge with the ground falling away on either side – left to the Thames and right to the Fairmile (A423). Beyond are wooded hills, and solitary trees (oak, lime and chestnut) enhance the meadows. The Mount, a large but alas no longer particularly attractive mound, is on your right.

The track slowly descends, opening up a view of the two valleys converging at Henley. This is a good place to sit and stare. The Chiltern landscape is outstanding here, and the Oxfordshire Way is nearly at its destination. You come down the hill to a kissing gate and into a wood of small mixed trees and bushes. The path drops quickly through this, does a left and right kink and emerges into a field. Here the outskirts of Henley and the noise of the A423 are close. Follow the hedge down, and climb over a stile on to the main road turning left for the town centre and the River Thames.

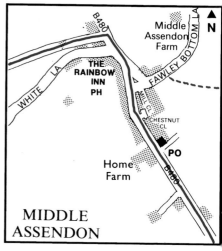

MIDDLE
ASSENDON

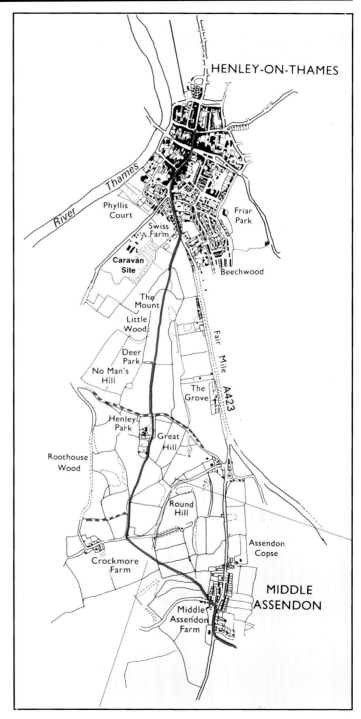

Henley-on-Thames

Henley-on-Thames

It is fitting that the Oxfordshire Way should end in this beautiful town upon the bank of the Thames, England's most famous river. You have encountered along your way many of the little streams and rivers that flow into the Thames, and here you can stand upon the noble Henley Bridge and look upstream towards far distant Gloucestershire and down stream along the Regatta course to Temple Island and in imagination the great city of London.

Henley is worth a leisurely survey. Its brick and flint, red-tiled buildings cover a span of many architectural generations. The fine Chiltern setting, the broad river, the old wharves, the 'Angle on the Bridge', the numerous good Georgian houses and coaching inns, and the excellent variety of modern shops all speak of centuries of quiet prosperity. For travellers such as yourselves there is a youth hostel (which you have passed on your right as you entered the outskirts of the town), many pubs and hotels, a railway station, and bus and coach services. Here you are about to leave the County of Oxfordshire, whose quiet beauty has we hope tempted you to return.

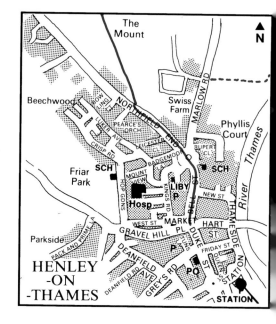

Notes

Notes

Notes

Notes

Notes

Notes

Notes

Notes